WHAT PEOPLE ARE SAYING ABOUT
MICHELLE MCKINNEY HAMMOND AND
WHEN SHIFT HAPPENS...

Recognizing that the only constant in life is change, Michelle deftly merges spirituality with practicality and provides actionable steps and winning strategies for moving forward, no matter what. *When Shift Happens* is guaranteed to ignite a fire in all who embrace the wisdom in these pages. I'll be reading it again and again.

—*Deborah Smith Pegues, CPA/MBA*
TV host; award-winning author of
30 Days to Taming Your Tongue

What a great book for the times we are in! Filled with practical insights and sound spiritual principles for navigating through changes in your life, Michelle assures us that whether we like it or not, shift will happen, but our response to it will make all the difference in the world. You will be inspired and empowered to make every shift count.

—*Roma Downey*
Actress, producer, and best-selling author

Perspective is what you see; perception is how you understand what you see. In this book, my friend, Michelle McKinney Hammond, helps us make sense of the seasons of life and teaches us how to transcend the cycles of life. This is pure gold!

—*Bishop Dale C. Bronner, D. Min.*
Author of *Power Principles*
Founder/senior pastor, Word of Faith Cathedral

The subtitle for *When Shift Happens* says it all! *Say Yes to Your Next!* should excite every reader and leader. You have a *next*; you want to say "yes" to it. My friend Michelle McKinney Hammond unpacks how to say yes to your next with huge doses of empathy, transparency, and pragmatic steps. You have a next, so run to it!

—*Sam Chand*
Leadership consultant
Author, *Leadership Pain*

As one who knows what believing looks like, I can tell you Michelle is the queen of reinvention. In this book, she shares rich insights and workable solutions with you that are sure to help you get your life back on track. A must-read if you're facing a change of any kind or just need a dose of inspiration.

—*The Honorable Sheryl Lee Ralph OJ*
Actress and singer

MICHELLE McKINNEY HAMMOND

WHEN SHIFT HAPPENS

SAY YES TO YOUR NEXT!

WHITAKER
HOUSE

WHEN SHIFT HAPPENS
Say Yes to Your Next!

michellehammond.com
relevancelife.org

ISBN: 979-8-88769-055-1
eBook ISBN: 979-8-88769-056-8
Printed in the United States of America
© 2023 by Michelle McKinney Hammond

Whitaker House
1030 Hunt Valley Circle
New Kensington, PA 15068
www.whitakerhouse.com

Library of Congress Cataloging-in-Publication Data (Pending)

1 2 3 4 5 6 7 8 9 10 11 Ⓦ 30 29 28 27 26 25 24 23

CONTENTS

Foreword.. 9

Acknowledgments 13

Introduction 15

FALL.. 23

    1. Life Happens 27

    2. Get Up 35

    3. Face the Facts... 47

WINTER.. 61

    4. Get Over It!.. 65

    5. Locate Yourself.. 75

    6. Make That Move 85

SPRING 97

    7. Keep Looking Up... 101

8. Forget About It!...109

9. Keep It Moving...117

SUMMER 129

10. Get Your Shift Together 133

11. Master the Cycle...147

12. What's Next? 159

13. All Shifts Matter...175

About the Author..185

As long as the earth endures, seedtime and harvest, cold and heat, summer and winter, day and night will never cease.
—Genesis 8:22 (NIV)

FOREWORD

It was June 2002. Much had shifted in my life in the previous six months. My mother had suffered a brain aneurysm while we were on the phone one night, which led to a series of life-shifting events in my family. When her life changed in an instant, so did mine. I went from being a single, carefree twentysomething pursuing her dream of writing and speaking to a caregiver trying to keep my business going while maneuvering the world of health insurance, doctors' appointments, and helping to raise a third grader who happened to be my only sibling.

I moved into my mother's home to help care for her. And as though divinely orchestrated, I had a nine-month stint filling in as cohost of a television show called *The Potter's Touch* with Bishop T. D. Jakes. The show was filmed at the church, a ten-minute drive from my mother's house south of Dallas. With the responsibilities of caregiving for my mother and my brother, then eight years old, this opportunity was about all I could handle at the time, and I was grateful. By June, I was shooting my last episode of the show. And it was one brief moment during that last shoot that created a major shift for my career as an author.

One of our guests on that episode was a kind, sharp woman named Cheryl Martin, a former news anchor for BET. I mentioned casually that I had written a proposal for my second book and was looking to get it published. As soon as the shoot ended, Cheryl was intent on striking up a conversation about my proposal. "Send me a copy," she said emphatically. "I have a friend who is an author, and her publisher is looking for authors like you. I will pass it along to her." It sounded a little too good to be true, and to be honest, I was slightly skeptical. I knew how rare it was to get an audience with a publisher because they have no lack of aspiring authors knocking on their door. It's even rarer for an author to pass along a proposal from someone they don't know. But Cheryl was persistent. She believed in me, even though we had just met. So I sent the proposal to Cheryl. Like she promised, she passed it on to her friend. A couple of weeks later, my literary agent called to say that Waterbrook Press, a division of Random House, was interested in my book.

So just who was that mystery friend Cheryl passed my proposal along to? Who was the friend who opened a door to a woman she didn't even know? That friend was a wholehearted, kind and generous author who has written over forty inspiring books and sold millions of them. In fact, this book you are reading is her latest. It would be a couple of years before I finally met Michelle McKinney Hammond at a women's conference where we were both speakers. From the moment my book proposal landed in her mailbox two decades ago until the writing of this foreword, our paths have intertwined at moments when a shift was occurring.

Shifts happen in moments. They can be divinely orchestrated. And they can change everything. I wrote five books with Waterbrook over the nine years following that first book deal with them. Later, when I became cohost of *Aspiring Women*, an Emmy-winning television show Michelle had cohosted for a decade, I interviewed her for the show from her fabulous Chicago apartment. Soon, we'd both experience unplanned shifts in our lives as I went through divorce, and she embarked on a transcontinental move to Ghana. During that time, I listened and encouraged her, and she did the same for me. As my life has transitioned to a blessed marriage, family, and business, Michelle still cheers me on. Her encouraging spirit shines just as brightly in the pages of this book.

Shifts go much better when we have friends to lean on. Even more so when those friends keep pointing us to God and reminding us He is there, guiding us if we choose to get quiet and listen. When those same friends cheer us on as we find our way in a new season and celebrate when our lives blossom in new ways, it is truly sweet. And I know that Michelle is cheering you on with as much enthusiasm as she cheers me on.

You are about to take a journey through these pages with a resilient, loving, faith-filled woman who wants you to live your life to the fullest. She will show you how to lean on God's wisdom for the answers you need and how to show up courageously when it's time to enter a new season, whether you have been welcoming that season or rejecting it. You will gain clarity and confidence in the process. Here's what I have learned about saying "yes" to your next:

1. Expect to feel afraid. It's normal.

Fear makes us want to stop moving forward. But the key to pushing through fear when change scares us is to expect it. Fear is normal. It's the reason Scripture tells us repeatedly to "be strong and courageous." So just know that the fear you are feeling means you're human. Your job in the face of fear is to be courageous. Let go of the expectation that the fear has to disappear in order for you to move forward. Whatever you need to do, do it in spite of your fear.

2. Look for the divine message.

God is speaking to you right now. It's why you decided to get this book. You are looking for answers to your current dilemma. God has them. In fact, He's speaking to you through your circumstances. Look for the message. Then heed it.

3. Know that God often works through people.

Just as Cheryl and Michelle used their power to open the door to a shift for me, God will also allow you to cross paths with those who will be instrumental in your shift. Sometimes we pray and expect a miracle but ignore the people who are a conduit for that miracle. Ask God to connect you with people He trusts and wants to place in your life for a purpose.

4. Pray for wisdom.

The right shifts occur when we make wise decisions. James 1:5 (NIV) promises, *"If any of you lacks wisdom, you should ask God."* Don't lean on your own understanding but seek God for His understanding in your situation and His wisdom in handling it.

5. Be bold and courageous.

When your new season comes, it is natural to want to hold on to the old season. It's familiar. So even when you want something new, you will still crave the certainty of what is familiar. This is when you will need to find your courage. Be bold and courageous. Blessings are on the horizon. Your courage will unlock them. I'm praying and rooting for you!

Grace and peace,
Valorie Burton
Founder, Coaching and Positive Psychology Institute

ACKNOWLEDGMENTS

To the best agent on the planet, Chip MacGregor, thank you for never giving up on me, encouraging me, and always being there for me. It means more than I can write or say.

To Christine Whitaker, Amy Bartlett, Peg Fallon, and the entire Whitaker House family, thank you for making me feel at home, giving me a space to express what God has put on my heart, and being committed to excellence.

To all my inner circle, who have pushed me up hill after hill and never let me stop or quit! You know who you are. Know that you are loved and appreciated to the moon and back. Or is it to the Son? Well, you know what I mean. I love you high, deep, and wide!

God, what would I do without You? I pray I never find out! Thank You for being there through all the seasons.

INTRODUCTION

*A person may have many ideas concerning God's plan for his life, but
only the designs of God's purpose will succeed in the end.*
—Proverbs 19:21 (TPT)

In light of certain events playing out in the lives of everyone on a global scale—the COVID-19 pandemic, the lockdown of the world, upheavals in economies, changes in businesses and all services, and educational and religious sectors—we are all aware that whether we are ready or not, shift happens.

Where were you when the world shifted? I was on my way to England for several speaking engagements. What started off as a normal routine would change the course of my life forever. I had anticipated a fun stay in the country with friends for a few days before venturing into the city to the hotel where I would remain during my speaking tour. However, the day after I landed, the country went into lockdown! Speaking engagements canceled! Ghana, the country where I was residing, locked its borders for seven months. A five-day stay in the country with friends turned into a five-month sojourn. The last two months, I moved into my own flat, not knowing how much longer I would have to remain in London.

Glued to the television and social media every day, I tracked what was happening in the world in a state of awe and wonderment. The world fell silent. I felt as if I were in a cocoon of sorts while taking quiet walks, musing about the future, how current events would affect it, and how long this was going to last... On and on, my mind was filled with a myriad of thoughts, in between wondering where all of this was taking me, the world, and those I knew and loved. As the death toll climbed and it became evident the end would not be clearly in sight for quite some time, I now had to shift gears—yes, there is that word again. I had to shift from waiting for the present trial to be over to deciding how I was going to navigate through it.

Though this situation seemed to be extreme, forcing me to make decisions I wouldn't have previously, it was my present reality. I had a decision to make. I could be paralyzed by it or take advantage of it. I chose the latter. While discovering the world of Zoom and alternative ways to reach out to and positively impact others, I came to the realization that, yes, life may demand that you shift against your will, but how you respond to its demands has everything to do with your outcome...for better or worse. That same choice is available to you too, hence this offering. I invite you on my journey, which is also *your* journey. So, let's walk it out together.

We live in a world that doesn't prepare us for the future. For change. Yet the shifting sands of time demand that we learn how to stand even when it feels as if we are losing our footing. It's been said that "life happens" and indeed it does. Faster than we expect or would prefer. I've seen it and experienced it. One day, you are hot; the next day, you are not. Cycles of thriving give way to merely surviving. Financial affluence gives way to seasons of leanness that leave you praying for daily bread.

What is the difference between those who flounder and those who flourish in the seasonal transitions of life that confront us as time marches on? It's the ability to understand and address the season you are in and assess its purpose. Clinging to the past stops us from having the future that awaits us. Life is an ongoing process. What appears to be the end is never the end. That roadblock, that failure, or that seeming denial is merely a detour to your next!

Your partner leaves you. What next? You suffer from financial fallout. What next? Your business fails. Your job ends. A loved one dies. The parents you know and love are now in need of your care. Life as you know it is no longer the life you knew and mastered… What next? What do you do when life seems to slow to a halt? When the things that worked before stop working. When the phone stops ringing. When you experience rejection, betrayal, or denial. When the demand for what you did slows to a trickle or is no longer there. You feel irrelevant, voiceless, obsolete. What then?

Does it mean you no longer have a purpose? A reason to keep on living or dreaming? Absolutely not! The challenge now becomes how to navigate your new season from a new perspective in order to complete your mission or even extend it. I call it getting past your "why" to your "because." Your "because" becomes the driver, urging you forward, sometimes even against your best inclinations. It reminds you of your passion, the first word or promise God whispered to your spirit, and the reason for moving forward in the face of opposition or even seeming defeat. Those who get stuck on "why" remain paralyzed, like the man at the pool of Bethesda in the Bible, watching the stirring around him but never quite grasping how to get in the flow and move forward. (See John 5:2–9.)

In the business world, moving forward past obstacles is called change management. In our personal world, we call it making the necessary adjustments. In the spirit realm, it's called, *"Forgetting the past and looking forward to what lies ahead, I press on to reach the end of the race and receive the heavenly prize for which God, through Christ Jesus, is calling us"* (Philippians 3:13–14).

In the kingdom of God there is no such thing as retirement—which suggests getting tired all over again (re-tire, get it?)—just higher levels of engagement in God's kingdom purpose. Purpose has no expiration date. But purpose demands we change with the seasons. The lies the enemy of our soul tells us when changes occur in our lives, leading us into unfamiliar terrain, can paralyze and stagnate us.

Fact: There is always a next! Our insistence that things remain the same in the face of things we can't control brings a disheartenment that causes us to question our worth and begin to compare ourselves to those who seem to be progressing without effort.

The end of an era as you know it is an amazing opportunity to discover new dimensions of yourself and your ability to reinvent yourself. An honest assessment and appreciation of the seasons of life help you to transition and weather each twist and turn with grace. Nothing comes to stay; it all comes to pass. And in the passing, a way is made for something new and greater to emerge.

Like the natural seasons, each shift is significant. Each season has a purpose that ultimately produces newness of life. Each stage is necessary, though they don't all look the same.

Imagine seeing someone walking down the road in a bikini in the middle of winter! Or someone taking a stroll on the hottest day of the year in a fur coat! You would think that something was very wrong, that they were in denial of the season they were in. To be in denial of change is to refuse to grow, to fail to produce greater fruit than you did before, and to miss the reward that awaits.

This book is all about personal change management. It's about helping you recognize which season you are in and how to navigate through that season without panicking. It's about seeing the light at the end of the tunnel and running toward it with the expectation that something phenomenal awaits. It's not over until the fat lady sings, or you decide to stop living, stop using the gifts within you, or stop sharing who you are and what you possess with the world around you. Navigating change is what you choose to make it. We all have the same ability to either respond strategically when life surprises us or react negatively and remain stuck.

The difference between those who rise to reinvent their lives and those who crumble under the pressure of shifting winds is found in a decision: The decision to live in spite of conditions. To stop making excuses and justifying paralysis. To literally take up your bed and walk against your worst fears.

Life can start again. And here's the exciting part: it can be better than it was before! What was is past, and so much more awaits. So, raise yourself up to your full height and declare with confidence, "Next!"

When you are at the top, be careful of the monster called PRIDE.

Pride will make you look down on the people who haven't attained your level of success.

When you are at the bottom, be careful of the monster called BITTERNESS.

Bitterness will make you jealous and think that other people are the reason you haven't made it.

When you are on the way to the top, be careful of the monster called GREED.

Greed will make you impatient and make you steal or seek shortcuts.

When you are on your way down, be careful of the monster called DESPAIR.

Despair will make you think it's all over, yet there is still hope.

—Carl Wauchope, City of Refuge New York Live

FALL

Boston made a name for itself not just for great seafood but also for the fall season when the leaves change color so brilliantly that it has become a tourist attraction. When things begin to change around us, we can either make it a positive attraction or a negative repellant. Change can either be a distraction or a projection forward.

Fall signals that the air is about to change; it becomes a period of transition, affording you not only a time of completing the remains of harvest but also the luxury of getting ready for winter. Some welcome the change in climate as a reprieve from the heat. Others begin to dread the onset of winter.

How we choose to assess change and make the necessary adjustments will ultimately impact how we move forward and whether we perish, survive, or thrive. Now is the time to ask several key questions that will enable you to move forward without fear.

- What is happening?
- What do I want to happen?

- What are my options?
- What is the worst thing that could happen?
- What is the best thing that could happen?
- What do I need to do to make a positive transition a reality?

I believe we know change is coming long before it occurs. There is what I call a *divine discontent* that starts in the pit of your stomach, on the edge of your subconscious, that begins whispering that where you are and what you are doing is no longer sustainable. Something needs to shift. What is right now has worn out its welcome. Like the leaves that change color before they fall, you feel yourself and the circumstances around you fading from their former glory. You feel a strange sense of detachment, a lack of passion, a lack of desire to keep doing the same thing. Like a battery-run toy, you move slower and slower before coming to a complete stop, out of power, and unable to function.

The problem is that even though we feel ready for change, the actual manifestation of it can be quite disconcerting, especially if the change was not orchestrated by us. We want to be in control and yet we rarely are when an actual shift begins to occur.

You may notice that none of the questions I listed asked how you *felt*. That is because now is not the time to discuss feelings. The range of emotions you may experience will most likely not help you navigate as you should. Apprehension, fear, doubt, anger, and pain will distract you, preventing you from making good decisions. Moving forward, you will have to master your thoughts and instruct your emotions to follow, not the other way around. Therefore, it is critical to make informed choices based on reality versus your response to it.

Let's look at some critical issues one must assess to recognize the signs of the season and navigate impending shifts that birth change. Keep in mind it's never the end. There is always a next!

*For everything there is a **season**, a time for every activity under heaven. A time to be born and a time to die.*
A time to plant and a time to harvest. A time to kill and a time to heal. A time to tear down and a time to build up.
—Ecclesiastes 3:1–3

ONE

LIFE HAPPENS

Years ago, I found myself facing massive life changes. Financial fallout. My career seemingly screeching to a standstill. Losing my home and my office. The death of my father. All in a Job-like succession!

I didn't sit down and cover myself with sackcloth and ashes like Job did. (See Job 16:15.) I couldn't afford to! I had to make some radical decisions to stay above the circumstances. The luxury of feeling sorry for myself didn't exist. I had to figure out how to make life work. But where to begin was the question. Putting one foot in front of the other took more energy than ever, but I had to keep moving! I had to keep hope alive. Failure was not an option.

It is inevitable. *Shift happens.* Why? Because growth demands change. Nothing greater can happen if we are not compelled by shifts and changes around us as well as within us. God knows that it is a human tendency to bask in complacency if we are left to our own devices. Even when we don't like our lives, the devil you know is better than the one you don't. We find excuses to stick with the status quo and try to ride it out on a sinking ship.

If you're honest, you've been here before, just with different characters and circumstances.

We mistakenly think that we are alone in our situation and that where we are will last forever, whether good or bad. Neither condition for anyone is rare or permanent. Both affluence and lack go through shifts and seasons of up and down. The stock market is proof of that. From bear to bull and back again. If only we could incorporate the principle of buying low and selling high in every aspect of life! Inevitably, what goes up must come down, and what goes down can only go so far before making the adjustment to rise again.

This is where faith comes into play. Fear and faith are both currencies that will purchase your result. Both are belief systems! They both produce what you choose to focus on. So, which one will you choose to bargain with: fear that it's over for you or faith that this setback is merely a setup for an amazing comeback? Your currency of choice—whether fear or faith—will determine how you spend your time and energy. Will you be distracted or determined? Either option will decide your emotions, attitude, beliefs, language, and actions. Your emotions will have everything to do with what you choose to believe based on the thoughts that generated your feelings. Once you've settled into agreeing with your emotions, you will make decisions that lead to actions, positive or negative. Those actions have everything to do with your outcome!

RECOGNIZE THE SEASON

The biggest mistake one can ever make is to assume that things won't change. It is easy to believe this when you're in a euphoric state of accomplishment, when you're on a roll. But many one-hit wonders have discovered the painful truth that life and the public are very fickle.

When I worked in advertising, one of our mantras was "You are only as great as your last ad."

Thus, there is a need for constant recognition of the times and the flexibility to make the necessary adjustments to remain relevant. Once this is mastered, your latter days can indeed be greater than your former because of the constant improvements you are making in your life, your craft, your relationships, and everything pertaining to every area of your life!

I previously mentioned divine discomfort. This is one of the first signs that shift is in the wind. I remember the day and time I thought to myself, in the midst of a flourishing advertising career, that there had to be something more. Yes, I was having a blast flying to New York and Los Angeles, rubbing elbows with the top creatives and celebrities in the field, and having access to all the glamourous events as I was being courted for business. I was the hotshot art director, copywriter, and producer on the block. *The golden girl.* Yet something was missing... There had to be more to life than designing ads that made people thirsty for a Coca-Cola, hungry for a Big Mac, or lusting after a Mustang. Something more... But what was it? Would I have the courage to step out and try something new? What would be next?

Admittedly, I was quite comfortable (although bored) in my career at that point. I had literally been there, done that. Been everywhere, done everything, met everyone. Yet I did not have the courage to step out into the unknown to discover what would really make my heart sing. Why? Because I really didn't know what that was! I had inklings, but nothing concrete. Nothing that I could solidly grasp and say, "Yes! This is what I want to do with my life!" The small nugget of a dream was there but how to make money and keep my current lifestyle escaped me. These things kept me rooted to the spot. Too paralyzed to move forward. I kept talking myself into being happy where I was. After all, I was the envy of many. The evidence of the struggle inside me was not evident to them. But the little whisper was gaining a louder voice.

Then it happened. I got fired! Yes, fired! Again, a mixture of emotions swept over me. I was scared because my first thoughts were about how this would affect me financially and professionally. Then I felt relief because perhaps now I could pursue those dreams...whatever they were. My boss told me as much.

"Michelle," she said, "we had to make a decision on who to let go and I chose you because I felt you were the one most likely to succeed if I released you."

Wow!

"I know you have other dreams," she continued, "but you've grown comfortable and content, and you'll never do anything different as long as you are here, so I'm kicking you out of the nest so that you can begin to fly."

Some people told me it was the nicest firing in the history of...well, firing.

Was I upset? No, I had felt it coming. Not being fired, exactly, but definitely moving on. I had even dreamt about it in vivid technicolor down to what one of my best friends was wearing when I stepped out of her office! Ironically, I had told them about the dream several days before I was fired, and everyone collectively pooh-poohed the idea that I could ever be fired because I was so good at what I did. Yet the feeling that the inevitable was about to occur was so strong that I had begun to pack up my office and take a few choice things home! When coworkers asked about this, I simply said that I felt the need to clean my office and organize my space better. Imagine their shock when I announced that what I had sensed had now become a reality.

Did I kick into action and pursue my dream right away? Of course not! Let's face it, although many of us long for change, we cling to the familiar. So, you guessed it, the first thing I did was try to find another job just like the one from which I had been removed.

I am saying "removed" because I believe the universe listened to my heart and not my head. Yes, life will create circumstances to make you align with the reason you were created seemingly without your assistance! What you see as the end is merely a detour on God's map. It is the path to your next.

OUT OF THE COMFORT ZONE

Like Jonah in the belly of the fish, I had been spewed out of my comfort zone so I could complete my divine assignment. Yet I was attached to my conventional ideas of how to make that happen. After all, I believed it should not feel foreign or require extra measures. I wanted my transition to be comfortable.

The word *comfortable* is quite illustrative. We tend to sit at a table that doesn't disrupt our comfort, even if we don't like what is being served. So, we add seasoning and try to change the flavor of what we are eating. We prefer minimal adjustments over leaps of faith. Past needs and present emergencies can cause you to rationalize finding another mode of living the same way. That is where we can find ourselves stuck even though a more exciting life awaits.

To be perfectly honest, my concern about my financial future short-circuited my dreams of a future in which I would write books and become an accomplished author. What if it didn't happen? How quickly could I earn an income? What would be next after that? My lack of clarity caused me to cling to the familiar, which no longer wanted to claim our friendship. And that is when I became stuck for a season.

Can I get a witness?

Fact: There is a tension between who we once were and who life is pushing us to become. The unfamiliar challenges the familiar, and we are left standing in the middle, trying to decide our preference even though we may have no choice!

Life can become harsh and impatient when it is time to shift. How can you know the season is changing? Simple. The old avenues close. You can't reach the same people. The old way no longer works. Life as you knew it is no longer sustainable, attainable, or desirable. You can bang your head against an unyielding wall, insisting life has to go this way when all the signs are pointing elsewhere, or you can choose to recognize the leaves are turning. The landscape of life no longer looks the same. These are all keys to knowing it's time for a change.

WHEN SHIFT HAPPENS

Take the time to consider where you are and what is happening or not happening for you at this moment. Assess what you desire and your present reality.

MINDSHIFT

- How would you assess your season?
- What stops you from doing something new?
- What are your options?
- How will you capitalize on what is at hand?

HINDSIGHT

Many are not prepared for the next season because they did not anticipate that anything different would occur. Many eat all of their harvest in the fall, not preparing for winter. Always be ready for your next, not out of fear but out of practicality. Even nature stores up for the winter so that it can comfortably ride out the cold.

Ask yourself this question: If money were not an issue for you, what would you be doing right now?

THE NEXT PRAYER

*Even the stork in the sky knows her appointed **seasons**, and the dove, the swift and the thrush observe the time of their migration. But my people do not know the requirements of the* Lord.

(Jeremiah 8:7 NIV)

Dear heavenly Father, I am struggling with the season I am in. I confess that fear has overwhelmed me and blinded me to my options and has also drowned out Your voice. I am struggling to find my footing. I waver between trusting You and taking life into my own hands. I confess I was not prepared for what has occurred, so forgive me for my lack of foresight. I need to know

Your requirements as well as Your instructions for this season. I am seeking Your wisdom as well as Your assurance that I will make it through this challenge. I am beyond figuring this out. I need Your light. I need Your strength. Teach me Your ways and increase my understanding. Help me to hear Your voice. Lead me and guide me. I extend my hands to You and await Your word, in the name of Christ Jesus. Amen.

What do you think the Lord requires of you at this time?

_____

_____

_____

_____

What has caused you to hesitate in taking the needed steps to move forward?

_____

_____

_____

_____

Write your faith confession here:

_____

_____

_____

_____

TWO

GET UP

There was a man who found himself in a stagnant predicament that lasted for thirty-eight years! (See John 5:2–15.) Thirty-eight years is a long time to be stuck in one position. One should wonder what would cause such complacency that he would settle into such a miserable space. There had been windows of opportunity for him to change his condition and yet he missed those chances and blamed his current situation on the lack of help to better his position. He apparently had lost all hope and saw no way around his predicament. He decided that was his lot in life and he might as well get used to it. At that point, all survival instincts were diminished to a state of apathy and resignation.

Yet it took just one voice, one command, to trigger something in this man that caused him to rise above his paralysis and be mobilized to change his circumstances. This voice of reason made no room for excuses or self-pity; instead it encouraged this man to command his state of being and left no room for compromise. *"Jesus said to him, 'Get up!'"* (John 5:8 NIV). And He further told the man to pick up the mat he had been lying on lest he be tempted to return to his former posture, mentally and physically.

That mat signifies all of the excuses we make in life for staying in the same position, doing the same thing, hanging around the same people who do not profit us or move us forward mentally, spiritually, physically, and yes, even financially. Our mind plays tricks on us. It wants change yet it's fearful of what must be implemented in order to make it happen. It questions whether we have the capacity to do what's necessary and frets over how our attempts will be received. It worries about the future, replays the past, and bemoans the present.

Therefore, I don't suggest that you listen to your heart. It is fickle and deceptive at best. It will cause you to look the blessing straight in the face… and then look past it because your eyes prefer to stay focused on something that is out of reach to justify your frustration.

During the pandemic, many chafed under the weight of the "Great Lockdown," as I came to call it. They moaned about the lack of activity and being stuck in the house with people they were quickly discovering they did not like! They longed for the freedom to move about, socialize, go shopping, do business, and enjoy the normal aspects of life.

On the flip side of that, others became highly creative, inventing new ways of communicating and doing business that caused them to thrive during a time of immobility! A latent company called Zoom literally zoomed (pardon the pun) to the forefront of the world at large as many discovered a new way to interact, and yes, even market their trade to higher profitability than before.

As churches took to the airwaves via social media, they discovered many more people were attending online than in their physical buildings, and giving went up; some pastors were heard saying they didn't need to go back to church! Though they missed the fellowship, they were achieving greater outreach electronically.

What was the difference between those who found themselves dying on the vine while feeling incarcerated versus those who were flourishing in the midst of "famine"? Their mindset. Those who chose to examine all options and take advantage of them prospered. They chose to see the desert landscape before them as a garden with endless opportunities to be fruitful. They had the audacity to say, "Thank you, COVID-19, I couldn't have done this without you!" Those who dared to think outside the box struck gold and expanded their horizons—while others gave in to their perceived chains and suffered.

Fact: People get stuck. Several things contribute to this, including where we are, self-perception, and the other voices we allow to affect our thought processes. We get stuck on one formula for getting things done, and when it doesn't work, we fail to see past it.

THE WAKE-UP CALL

COVID-19 was a wake-up call for me to reinvent myself. After I arrived in London, the day before the great lockdown began, I discovered I couldn't go home because the borders of Ghana were closed until further notice—to the tune of seven months! As I sat in London far away from home with nothing more at my fingertips than a welcoming family, a beautiful home, a cuddly dog, the glorious English countryside, and my computer, it would have been easy to languish and do absolutely nothing. I confess I did that for several weeks and enjoyed every minute of it. Ironically, I had prayed and told God I needed at least two weeks to do absolutely nothing because I was exhausted, drained, and running on empty, feeling I had nothing left to give. I welcomed the time of refreshment, relaxation, and restoration. I also knew there was only so much time for doing nothing. Something had to kick in…but what?

I could have used a thousand excuses for continuing to languish in nothingness. I needed to be in my office to get anything done. My staff was far away. I had no speaking engagements. Blah, blah, blah! Everything that could have been a problem presented a new opportunity to find an innovative solution.

"Why don't we try doing one of those online hangouts we've discussed for forever?" suggested Tega, my daughter from another mother.

"Okay," I decided, "what do we have to lose?"

It turned out we had everything to gain as hundreds logged on from around the world when the *MMH Hangout* was launched. I became the conduit for hundreds of women and a few lucky men to meet and connect, form new friendships, network in a safe place, and hear from amazing guests who shared their keys to living, loving, and overcoming. So many great connections were formed, and a growing network of people gathered and were empowered to live the lives they dreamed about. It became a place of safety, comfort, and celebration that continues today!

I discovered the world was at my fingertips from the luxury of my room! Would I have ever done the hangout if I wasn't constrained to one location? Probably not. We had discussed it but never done it before because... Why? Because I was too busy doing all the other things I was used to. But now that I was no longer able to operate at my usual capacity, necessity became the mother of new inventions—like the *MMH Hangout*, curriculum for online courses, and recording online books. I even took online courses, expanded my knowledge base, and got my coaching certification. Suddenly I was busier than I had been when I had the freedom to run around.

There are times when we don't realize that our freedom can be the worst distraction and hindrance to true productivity. Confinement caused me to focus.

Like the paralyzed man at the pool of Bethesda that I referenced earlier from the Gospel of John—my favorite book in the Bible—I could have been paralyzed and panicked about how I was going to operate and earn a living. Instead, my mind shifted from "I *have* to stay in the house" to "I *get* to stay in the house!" What a difference my mindset made. Suddenly, I was no longer confined! *Getting to* versus *having to* opened a world of possibilities for me. Now I could take advantage of my situation rather than being mastered by it.

NO EXCUSES

Recognizing the season and getting rid of excuses was critical in this timeframe. Perhaps God was using this time to expand me beyond my self-imposed boundaries. Stretch me beyond my comfort zone. Cause me to grow, to become more fruitful and effective. I took the time to silence my spirit and remove myself from all of the speculations and conspiracy theories on social media to discern what was really going on. What could be gleaned from where I was? I do not believe in operating "under the circumstances." I prefer to look for ways to triumph despite them. This is where I want you to readjust your mindset. You are not a victim; you are a victor! What do you have to work with? I had a computer. You may only have a voice, a hammer, a pen and paper, an idea… whatever you have, it's the seed of something great.

Fact: The only difference between someone who has an idea and someone who takes that idea and succeeds is that the latter decided to do something with what they had. They found a way to make it work! Making it work involves bettering the lives of others while prospering yourself. Not just monetarily but emotionally, mentally, physically, and spiritually.

There are different ways that we get stuck: physically, geographically, relationally, mentally, emotionally, and even spiritually. Actually, one can lead to the other if we are not careful. Many years ago, I was hit by a car. Never one to stop moving, I was horrified to find myself incapacitated for over a year. Three surgeries, endless physical therapy sessions, and having to learn how to walk again was an overwhelming and draining experience. Lying in bed with my knee strapped to a machine that kept it moving constantly to prevent the development of keloids or excessive scar tissue, I could have given into being as dysfunctional as I felt. However, I had friends—rather opinionated friends—who had a truckload of suggestions about what I should be doing with my life and the *opportunity* my misfortune afforded me.

"What do you think God is saying to you about what you should be doing?" they asked. To which I answered, "I haven't the slightest idea. Pass the Tylenol please." They were not deterred by my pain or my mental state. They stayed on my case until one of them said, "What about that book you started writing a few years ago? Now would be the time to finish it while you are stationary." Hmmm, that was a nice way of putting my state of being. Not only did she suggest this, but she also followed through by appearing at my home on several Sunday afternoons to draft and send proposals to various publishing houses while I propped myself up in bed to finish writing the book on my computer.

The rest is history. By the time I graduated to crutches, I was meeting with an acquisition editor from a large publishing house. Now, forty-two books later, I am still standing to tell the story. What happened? The power of my network happened. If it's true that "bad company corrupts good manners," it is also true that "your network can affect your net worth."

THE COMPANY YOU KEEP

The company you keep can have a deep impact on your life and the decisions you make. There is a reason why rich people only hang out with rich people. Together they grow richer as they influence one another with information, strategies, and keys to gaining more wealth. Misery loves company, and there is nothing like a good pity party, but nothing will come of it but a greater sense of failure.

The importance of gaining wisdom is cited several times in the book of Proverbs, which illustrates two personas, *wisdom* and *folly*. It is interesting that they both have the same access to you and their invitation to align with them is also the same. However, responding to one or the other produces entirely different results. *Wisdom's* invitation leads to life, while folly's invite leads to a death that's not always physical. It can also be spiritual, emotional, mental, relational, professional, financial, and more. Something dies or flourishes whenever we make choices. This is why we must be discerning about our alignments and influences.

The paralyzed man who spent his days lying by the pool in John 5 was not there alone. He was surrounded by friends like himself with various physical ailments—blind, lame, and immobile. There was a consensus among them that they would remain in this state forever. Only the one who dared to seize the moment when the fabled healing waters were stirred was energized and healed. But resignation played a vital part in halting even the effort to receive healing.

I encourage you to examine your friendships, inner circles, and alignments. It has been scientifically proven that your life will look like that of your three closest friends. Yikes! What does that look like for you?

What conversations are you feeding off? Like food, you consume your words and others' words, and they become a part of your system, affecting your health mentally and physically.

We live off words fed into our spirits, our minds. Every word that we hear, we digest, and this regulates our thoughts, attitudes, beliefs, and finally our words, choices, and actions. Language is so powerful; it speaks things into existence—life or death, joy or sorrow, strength or weakness, productivity or stagnation… You get to choose!

Fact: You are not only what you eat; you are also the company you keep. The things that you allow to talk you into and accommodate the paralysis that hinders you from embracing your shift must be banished.

As I mentioned earlier, it took one voice to cut through all of the other voices this man at the pool of Bethesda had been listening to in order for something different to occur in his life. One voice cut through the excuses. One voice silenced all the incorrect conclusions. Deep within yourself, you know what you were created for. That you are bigger and greater than your *seeming limitation.* It only takes one voice that resonates with the truth within you to give you the courage to *rise* to the occasion.

YOU ARE YOUR THOUGHTS

That paralyzed man had the capacity to stand all along. He didn't need to do what the others thought they needed to do to walk. It took heeding the right counsel.

The voices that surround you can shut you down even if they mean well. They will hand you the ammunition for your excuses and exchange your faith for fear and doubt. It is all a matter of mindset—the mindset that generates from language and wrong confessions. The things that repeat themselves over and over in your subconscious can war against your conscious mind and win the battle if you let it. It is said that our subconscious mind controls 95 percent of our life. And yet your subconscious can be realigned and designed to agree with your spirit, which has the unlimited capacity to not only dream but empower you to achieve what you visualize.

The subconscious mind does more than dream; it is also always awake because it controls all the vital processes and functions of the body. While the conscious mind sleeps, the subconscious mind is still fully awake, hearing and processing things while we sleep. The subconscious mind operates on habit and takes everything literally.

Did you know that the subconscious mind cannot differentiate between negative and positive thoughts? It is not subjective; it can't reason or think independently. It only obeys commands. It takes its commands from the conscious mind. In other words, you can have what you think and speak! This is why, in the Bible, God talks so much about controlling your thought life and directing your thoughts. (See, for example, Romans 12:2; Philippians 4:8.)

The other fascinating thing about the subconscious is that it only thinks in the present. The conscious mind dwells on the past and worries about the future, but the subconscious can only focus on the present moment. The subconscious mind is like a computer that processes huge amounts of information through your senses and translates it back to you in a flash. It does not analyze; it focuses on emotion versus logic and reason. Therefore, your emotions cannot be trusted. Things are not always what they seem.

Why do I share all of this with you? Because I want you to understand how critical your mindset is for navigating shifts and changes in life. Based on your thoughts, attitudes, and emotions, your outcome can vary from amazing to devastating. The choice is up to you. Again, you get to choose the voice you listen to and the actions that will follow. How your story ends is up to you.

Like a little girl who resists her father's admonishments to sit down after being forced to do so and then boldly declares, "I may be sitting down, but I'm standing up inside," you need to stand up inside. Stand up to your fullest God-given potential and produce what is already in you.

It is significant that the paralytic by the pool of Bethesda was told to not only get up but to take up his mat and walk, to follow through with the shift of mindset and get rid of everything that accommodated his former state. Have you ever rolled out of bed and been tempted to get back in? So many times, even our suffering becomes comfortable to us. In many cases, the situation we hate becomes *normal* to us to the point where we find ourselves longing for the thing we hate simply because it is familiar and feels safer than the unknown. We feel ill-equipped to begin to pursue our dreams, yet all we have to do is start. The best way to get to your *next* is to start where you are, with what you've got, no matter how insignificant it may seem. You don't have to wait for anyone to help you. Start by talking to yourself. Start by bolstering your willpower and fortifying yourself within. Start by believing in the force at work within you that makes up for all your deficiencies. You can do this! Just start with what you've got.

EXAMINE YOUR OPTIONS

I love the biblical story of Moses receiving instructions from God before he went to lead the children of Israel out of Egypt. When God asked him what was in his hand, Moses only saw a shepherd's staff. God told him to cast it down, and it turned into a serpent. (See Exodus 4:2–4.) Sometimes you have to cast down your *nothing* in order for it to become *something*. Let it go. Stop insisting on what it is and its purpose. Think outside of the box. See the endless options before you, the possibilities you never considered. Moses's brother Aaron threw down his staff, which turned into a powerful serpent that devoured all the staffs of the Pharaoh's magicians! (See Exodus 7:10–12.) Moses didn't see that coming but God's greater plan and power were revealed. He and Aaron discovered that they had the capacity to do greater things than they thought they were capable of.

What is in your hand?

Or how about the widow who was on the brink of financial ruination, about to have her sons taken away in slavery to pay her debts? (See 2 Kings 4:1–7.) The prophet Elisha encourages her to gather as many vessels as she can, shut the door behind her, and begin to pour the little bit of oil that she had into her neighbors' empty jars. The oil didn't stop flowing until she ran out of jars! I bet she wished she could find another pot or pan or something—anything in order to keep the oil flowing so she could have enough to sell and experience financial overflow.

Do you have the capacity to be blessed the way God wants to bless you? Are you preparing and making room in your life for the greater *next*? Are you willing to isolate yourself to increase your capacity to literally overflow in your giftings? God doesn't waste anything, so how much you are blessed is up to you and how you prepare and what you make room for. How willing are you to let your needs be made known to those who can help you? How confident are you to pour out what you have to enrich yourself on all levels?

WHEN SHIFT HAPPENS

It is a critical time to examine your circle, your influences, and the things that you randomly confess about your situation. Taking an aggressive stand against negativity and limiting beliefs is imperative. You may need to set new boundaries.

MINDSHIFT

+ Who is in your circle?
+ What are they saying about your situation?
+ What excuses are you making for your lack of action?
+ What are you afraid to release?
+ What limiting belief is hindering you from moving forward?

HINDSIGHT

You are what you eat and who you associate with. What are you ingesting audibly and visually? Conversations feed your system and your beliefs, leaving you stronger or weaker, nourishing you or depleting you, depending on what you are taking in. Words, experiences, and impressions are what you regurgitate in words that ignite the atmosphere around you and invite positive or negative energy and occurrences into your space. Time to change your diet!

Ask yourself this question: What are you eating?

THE NEXT PRAYER

*He changes times and **seasons**; he deposes kings and raises up others. He gives wisdom to the wise and knowledge to the discerning.*

(Daniel 2:21 NIV)

Dear heavenly Father, I confess that I have been paralyzed. I have relied on other sources and listened to other voices that only confused me further. I have placed my confidence in everything but You—I ask for Your forgiveness. I have tried my own way and failed miserably so now here I am. I have allowed worry to dominate my emotions and left no room for faith. I don't even know when I resigned myself to growing apathetic about my situation. But I realized the will to fight had left me and I had given into the opinion of others that this would be my lot in life. What an insult that must be to You. So now I look to You to deliver me and free me from my self-imposed bondage. Teach me Your ways; reveal Your thoughts toward me. I want to rest in the assurance that You care for me and that everything I now face will all work for the good in my life. Give me Your wisdom and increase my discernment. Help me not to make the mistakes I've made in the past. I am ready for my next. Lead me there, in the name of Christ Jesus. Amen.

Write what voices are keeping you from your next.

_____

_____

_____

_____

What new confession will you have?

_____

_____

_____

_____

Write your faith confession here:

_____

_____

_____

_____

THREE

FACE THE FACTS

The country was on lockdown. Their leader—the one directing their exodus from a hostile territory, where they had labored, into a new promised land flowing with freedom, milk, and honey—was dead. (See Deuteronomy 34.) Although they had been told that Moses would not make it to the promised land with them, sorrow mingled with confusion, paralyzing them and preventing them from moving forward. No one wanted to repeat the mistakes of the past. Fear of the unknown also loomed ahead.

Years before, when Moses had left them to seek direction from God for forty days, there had been lots of whispered discussions about what had happened The people had grown impatient; feeling abandoned, they had given in to their fears. Not knowing where to direct their faith, they had donated their jewelry to create and erect a golden calf to worship. (See Exodus 32.) It had made them feel anchored and secure, knowing that a god, no matter how inanimate, was in their midst. But their security had been short-lived. When their leader had returned, his anger had been unleashed as he'd cast down the tablets bearing instructions for the people from the real God. The mayhem that had followed was forever etched in their memories. The price of their unbelief had cost them dearly: lives were lost. The regrets of that day outlived their sorrow and their fears.

No, they didn't want to repeat that mistake. But what now? This time, Moses would not be returning. What would happen to all of their plans? As they reflected on the way forward, they were reminded of another grave mistake they had made in the past on their journey to this place. They had sent out spies to check out the land they had been promised, and these spies had come back with a report that engulfed the camp in fear. Yes, the promised milk and honey were there. Yes, there were huge grapes, pomegranates, and figs. But there were also giants in the land! (See Numbers 13.) Why hadn't God mentioned the giants? Doubt had overtaken their courage and rendered them completely incapable of moving forward.

God had been insulted. After all that He had done to prove Himself to them, from parting the Red Sea to delivering them from Pharaoh, they still had no faith. In his anger, He decided if they didn't trust Him, they could go no further. He would wait until a generation arose that had the capacity to look past challenges to claim the promise.

Had it not occurred to them that God didn't mention the giants because they were not an issue in His mind? They had already been given the land. They just had to move forward to claim it. Their unwillingness to press past their fears cost them dearly. They were left to wander aimlessly for forty years. Now a new generation that knew their history stood at the brink of claiming what had been foretold. However, Moses—the leader they knew and were used to—was gone, and Joshua stood in his place. Again, the people were on the brink of finalizing the achievement of what they had set out to do. They were too far gone to return to where they had come from, but too unsure of how to move into the future. The question resonated throughout the camp: What to do next?

STEPPING INTO NEXT

Moses's mantle of leadership had been passed to Joshua. He had been forewarned of his mentor's impending death but was still stymied by this development and not quite clear how to chart their course. He submitted to being still and gaining clarity. Would he have the respect and trust of the people? Did he really have what it took to get them where they wanted to go? Despite being one of the twelve spies sent into the land of Canaan, a victorious general in Israel's battle against their vicious enemies, the Amalekites, and handpicked by God to succeed Israel's long-time leader (see Numbers 13:16, Exodus 17:9–13, and Joshua 1:1–2, respectively), Joshua was riddled with self-doubt. God had to tell him several times to *"be strong and courageous"* (Joshua 1:6).

It took God Himself to call Israel to order. It was time to face the facts. Moses was dead, but the dream wasn't. There was still a promise to claim. Nothing had changed except that the one they thought would help them accomplish their goal was gone. Not to be callous, but there was still life to be lived and a mission to accomplish! It was time to shift and get on with the program.

The newly designated leader shook himself and accepted that it was now up to him to step up to the plate and complete the journey they had started. God told him:

> *This is my command—be strong and courageous! Do not be afraid or discouraged. For the* LORD *your God is with you wherever you go.*
>
> (Joshua 1:9)

Thus encouraged, Joshua snapped into taking charge. He rallied the troops and reassured them just as he had been reassured by God that they could do this! They could possess what had been promised.

Yes, mistakes had been made on the way to the promised land, but they would not be repeated. Their former leader was gone and would not be returning, but this time, the nation would not be turning to false gods as they previously had. Nor would they give into fear and confusion. They had learned that lesson. They were now all ears to hear God's instructions and their new leader's directions.

What are the false gods we tend to worship in search of assurance and security? Formulas, institutions, traditions, culture, generational habits, and yes, even longstanding relationships that do not serve us. They are like the law. Words that kill and do not give life.

Spies were again sent to check out the territory they were about to take, but this time, things were different. There was no doubt or fear. This time, they came back with a positive report that gave the people boldness, courage, and determination. (See Joshua 2.) They didn't know how the walls were going to come down, but they were ready to do what they had to do to claim their promised land. They followed the strange instructions of their leader, marching around Jericho for seven days. On the last day, the priests blew their shofars, and everyone shouted loudly. (See Joshua 6:1–20.) The Lord had given them odd instructions that perhaps no one understood, not even their fearless general. But it worked. Sometimes you have to do something you don't understand to get what you want.

THE LEAP OF FAITH

That is how faith works. It may not be able to decipher the science of it all. It may not understand the mystery of how vibration and sound can topple a formidable obstruction that stood between them and the territory they came to claim. All that was required was their obedience to take a risk, trusting for a positive outcome. This time, they would believe the spies' report. This time, they would do what they were told without whining or complaining. This time, they would smell the victory before they tasted it and dare to believe they would get the results they wanted. This is the stuff that transforms dreams into reality.

What appeared to be a peculiar act was rather strategic on God's part. Spirit and science merged to create a miraculous outcome. The entire nation of Israel consistently marching around the walls of Jericho for seven days in a row put pressure on the ground that caused anything not deeply rooted to lose its foothold. Adding the vibration from the shouting and the blasts of the rams' horns was the nail in the coffin for those walls.

How does this translate practically for us today?

Sometimes you must do something unusual for something different to happen. Sometimes you have to apply pressure to your situation. Create consistency in your habits that will break up the status quo in your life! Your words, your joy level, and what your system shouts to the world literally affect the atmosphere around you, shattering doubt and obstructions that impede your progress and removing obstacles from your life.

Whatever is in your way has to move as you advance in confidence, consistently, without fear.

The inhabitants of Jericho literally lived in fear for seven days as the Israelites marched around their city. It shifted the atmosphere within their walls to anticipate their defeat. By the time the walls fell, they had no fight left in them. They were defeated before the fight even got started. Sometimes the thing you fear is equally afraid of you!

What habits are you practicing that build momentum in your life that generates a successful outcome? What is your attitude? Do you anticipate victory? The Israelites appeared to be a motley crew who had been through a lot. Yet they did not let their past color their attitudes moving forward. They were used to being slaves and unestablished underdogs, but they were willing to do what it took to graduate to being overcomers.

THE LESSONS WE LEARN

It's been said that those who don't acknowledge their history are destined to repeat it. However, that same history can rob you of your future if it isn't seen from the right perspective. Let's face it, we all make mistakes. But that is not where failure lies. It's choosing not to learn from our mistakes that causes us to lack understanding or exercise discernment and wisdom when the opportunity is presented again. Trust me, it *will* come around again. You will get another chance to pass the test. God has determined certain things before the beginning of time, before our own existence.

Thank goodness the outcome of God's kingdom plan and purposes have far less to do with us than we think or believe. The cycles are repeated until they are completed in full alignment with God's divine design for the world and humanity. Yes, His will *will* be done despite us all! Certain facts must be faced if we are to accomplish the things that beat insistent rhythms in our hearts. I call that *God-given desire*. His desire given to you becomes your desire. When our hearts agree and we cooperate with His plan, it unfolds as it should—in the right time, right place, and with the right players in place.

The first thing you need to understand is that your past failures are in no way indicators of your future. This is the first step to getting past where you are. As a matter of fact, mistakes and failures hold valuable keys to success. They expose your weaknesses, the things you need to surrender; and they also help to redirect your focus.

As we learn our lessons from what has happened, we can create new milestones. Former difficulties become frameworks for an amazing acceleration to higher heights.

So begin by forgiving yourself. Face your reality and acknowledge your humanity.

The reality is that the things you did in the past may not work in the present. Yesterday's leader and leadership style may be out of touch and no longer relevant. There is a reason why the old guard gets changed. Sometimes the person or method that got you to a certain point may not be the one to carry you to completion. It may take another way of doing things, another person with greater insight into what needs to be done *next* to bring the full picture into focus. This is where companies that fail tend to go left after doing so many things right. Their insistence on being inflexible and not knowing when to embrace change robs them of success and relevance.

Knowing when to take a risk and try again is another area where many fall short. You tried it before, and it failed, so you won't try again. Ah, but now it is a new season, and *this* is not *that*.

Like the story of the discouraged fishermen who had fished all night without catching a thing.

> When [Jesus] had finished speaking, he said to Simon [Peter], "Now go out where it is deeper, and let down your nets to catch some fish." "Master," Simon replied, "we worked hard all last night and didn't catch a thing. But if you say so, I'll let the nets down again." And this time their nets were so full of fish they began to tear! (Luke 5:4–6)

A voice that these fishermen did not recognize or deem qualified to advise them told them what they needed to do. Grudgingly, or perhaps just to humor their unknown advisor and prove him wrong, they threw out their nets, which nearly broke because the catch was so plentiful. Input from a different perspective and a simple *shift* at the right time made all the difference. Just think of what they would have never experienced, the profit they would have lost, if they had failed to be open, lacking the flexibility and the capacity to try again!

Don't take the loss personally. It is there to instruct you and show you what you haven't learned yet. But also to show you what is available. Misdirection can be redirection, if we pay attention to the cues. When you are completing a maze on paper, if you hit a wall, you back up and try a different approach until you navigate yourself successfully from point A to point Z. Why not in life? Making a mistake is not an indictment against your intelligence. It is the gateway to broader understanding and accomplishment if you allow it to show you what you didn't see before.

Fact: The only giants we must worry about are the ones inside our minds. These imaginary hindrances make fear a reality and rob us of our personal victory. We become the greatest hindrance to our progress. The experiences of the past feed us false information about our future, stopping us from moving forward. Only when we choose to embrace pain and failure will we master our lives and find the freedom to live fearlessly, taking the risks we need to take to get to our *next*.

THE VALUE OF MISTAKES

Once, during a piano lesson, I kept pausing when I thought I was going to make a mistake. Finally, my instructor asked me why I was doing this. "I was getting ready to mess up," I said.

He told me, "So what? If you do it wrong, you will learn how to do it right. We will never complete the song if you keep that up!"

As I boldly plunged forward, I realized I made fewer mistakes because the fear was gone. The permission to fail freed me to try without inhibition. The fear had created a hesitancy that was not warranted for the exercise. My hesitation literally became a self-fulfilling prophecy as it set me up to fail as I anticipated. There are a couple acronyms we can use when thinking about how FEAR holds us back: False Evidence Appearing Real, or Faith Exiting Against Risk. Either way, fear has no place in the lane of progress.

Be willing to take a risk. Those who dare to embrace their *next* usually find themselves landing quite safely when they dare to make the leap.

Against their own misgivings, those fishermen who encountered Jesus listened to a stranger's advice. Be open to other voices yet discerning of who is speaking. Are their words filled with love, peace, empowerment, and sound direction, or laced with fear, doubt, anger, pain, and indecision? This is how you lift and separate the many voices you will hear. Consider the source and the effect of the counsel. Those who move on instinct, that feeling in your gut, can sometimes be considered a bit insane and yet at the core of us all is a *knowing* that simply seeks confirmation without, resonating with what is already within. God is kind enough to send that voice to lead you. You will know it when you hear it. That is the voice to follow. It will always lead to life and a better way.

Remembering why you set off in your present direction in the first place will help you complete your mission no matter what roadblocks may challenge you. For the joy set before you. That should be enough motivation to endure setbacks and despise the things that distract you while staying on course. Never give in, never give up. Nothing. Is. Worth. Giving. Up. No loss. No pandemic. No heartbreak. No disappointment. No rejection. No setback. Finish the course. Rest if you must. Scream if necessary. But keep it moving. Beat your chest. Courage up. Get bold and move forward. Feel the adrenaline rush of everything in your system saying, "Yes! I was born for this!"

Everyone hailed a runner who fell on the track during the 1992 Summer Olympics Games in Barcelona. Injured and disappointed, he got back up. With the assistance of his father, Derek Redmond continued until he had completed a full lap of the track as the crowd gave him a standing ovation.[1] Although he did not win, and official Olympic records list him as "Did Not Finish" because of the assistance he received, who do you think was the most remembered from that race? The winner or the one who limped across the finish line? You guessed it! The one who chose to endure and finish despite the pain. The glory came for him in another way. He ignited the hearts of everyone who has ever been tempted to quit.

---

1. For more on this runner's story and his career as a motivational speaker, visit derekredmond.com.

The biggest idol or false god of all is our perception of what we believe life and success should look like. At the end of the day, completing what we were created for is the highest mark of success. It is the thing that will give you all the joy, peace, and fulfillment you seek. It just may not be wrapped in the package that you expect.

Jesus said that in the last days, people's hearts will fail them out of fear. (See Luke 21:26.) When the winds of change come to challenge our beliefs and dismantle our normal way of doing things, those who are not flexible, faith-filled, or formidable will fall. Rigidity will cause you to break. Those who have the fortitude to embrace and navigate change will get to reap its rewards.

THE CATALYST OF INVENTION

As businesses found new ways to conduct business during the COVID-19 pandemic, many discovered they had been wasting money on overhead. The workforce in great part was working more effectively from home! Churches panicked initially when they couldn't gather, but they found innovative ways to reach a larger audience online. It was an electronic book of Acts taking place in a modern scenario. The church was being forced out into the mainstream, to touch those they would have never reached within four walls.

Portals of learning were opened online. Not only did schools take over the Internet, but a plethora of online courses were launched. Books sold at a greater pace than they had in decades. Online sales went through the stratosphere. Upheaval had birthed changes and created new businesses that no one would have considered before. It increased learning and progress. Shifts in how people did business, lived, and interacted were happening all around us even as there was no external movement. *The shift occurred inside*—inside our minds, homes, schools, business establishments, churches, and governments. Everyone was forced to look at how to do life and relationships differently. Some made the necessary adjustments and flourished, while others clung to the old and literally went belly up, dying on the vine.

It's true you can't put new wine in an old wineskin; it will swell and burst the skin, spilling its contents, and all will be lost. (See Matthew 9:17;

Mark 2:22; Luke 5:37–39.) New wine calls for a new way of containing it. A new way of doing what you did before. Take a deep breath and say to yourself, "Life happens, shift happens, and change is good."

WHEN SHIFT HAPPENS

There is never just one way to do things. The One who created you is bigger than that. When all of your preconceived ideas have failed, it is not over. It is merely an invitation to expand your understanding, your skills, and your faith. Learning to walk with open hands is both scary and exciting. It is the beginning of a great adventure to experience something new and perhaps encounter a miracle.

MINDSHIFT

+ What has not worked for you in the past?
+ What risk are you willing to take?
+ What change are you resisting?
+ What fear will you need to release to continue forward?
+ What options are presently within your reach?

HINDSIGHT

Our initial dreams are always true. However, they won't insist on manifesting if we are not willing to do the work it takes to birth them. It is not that it takes a long time for dreams to come true. Dreams simply wait for us to align with them and have the courage to take a risk.

Ask yourself this question: What is the secret desire or dream that I have suppressed until now?

THE NEXT PRAYER

Then you will know the truth, and the truth will set you free.
(John 8:32 NIV)

Dear heavenly Father, I confess that I falter when it comes to facing the truth of my predicament. It hurts too much. I think somewhere in the back of my mind if I don't acknowledge it, somehow it will go away or resolve on its own. I know that isn't true, yet I put off dealing with the truth of my situation. Help me to embrace the truth rather than fear it. You know me inwardly and outwardly. You know my mind, my heart, and my inclinations. You know my weaknesses and my strengths, even the secret things that I fear. I ask that You still my heart and give me the courage to embrace the truth about my situation, myself, and even about You. Sometimes I don't see You as I ought. I am suspicious of Your agenda and blame You for how my life is going. Today I choose to take responsibility. To face the facts and change my scenario by making a different choice. It's scary but I am ready for my next. My life is in Your hands, in the name of Christ Jesus. Amen.

What fact have you been avoiding about your situation?

_____

_____

_____

_____

What options do you have to change in order to deal with your truth in a constructive way?

_____

_____

_____

_____

Write a faith confession here:

_____

_____

_____

_____

WINTER

Cold. Seemingly barren. Winter can signal death to those who don't understand the purpose of each season. Dying can be more productive than merely existing because it sheds things that impede growth. We love to admire the butterfly. We talk about the caterpillar engulfing itself in a cocoon, but we don't go into detail. We don't discuss the fact that the caterpillar literally dies, liquifying itself before breaking out of its shell, spreading its wings, and taking flight! The moral of the story is you must die before you fly!

The winter of the soul can be a lonely place of isolation and darkness. It can cause you to question yourself. To question God. To question your life, your purpose, and your direction. Winter is known for having the shortest days and the longest nights. Fleeting sunlight that we chase in some regions of the world by manipulating time. Adjust your clocks for daylight savings time. Spring forward, fall back! That is the rule. Falling back is an attempt to take advantage of an earlier sunrise and finish the day before the sun sets, leaving people to navigate in the dark on the way home from school or work. Such is life. We try to shorten the time of difficulty by manipulating our circumstances until we are forced to face the darkness we can't escape as we run in search of light.

Winter is a time for turning inward and deep reflection. Some hibernate in winter, waiting for warmer weather, while others take advantage of winter sports as they celebrate cooler temperatures and the beauty of an amazing snowfall. Again, it's all in the way one looks at every given situation. Whether we retreat in depression or take advantage of the season with a sense of uninhibited celebration is up to us!

Death is a natural part of the cycle of life. Physically, spiritually, emotionally, professionally, financially, and relationally, in every realm of life, there is a time when things fall off by design or by deliberate action. We need to view this death, this loss, what we perceive as an ending, in the right light. The reality is it's never over, no matter what it is; whatever the situation, it is a detour to another level of life and experiences. This is our present hope that gives way to new life if we embrace this truth.

Take the time to reflect on where you are right now.

+ What do you need to surrender?

+ What has run its course in your life?

+ What have you been longing to change?

+ What actions have you resisted?

+ What is no longer sustainable?

+ What avenues have been closed to you that were formerly open?

The answers to these questions will reveal why you are experiencing a winter of the soul. Now is not the time to grow sad. It's time to get excited! Though it looks as if nothing is happening, a lot is going on beneath the surface. Hibernation leads to regeneration. Know that the light will come, revealing things that were hidden before that will equip you for your journey forward.

The nights are longer and the days are shorter in the wintertime. This translates into our lives as well. It seems as if the trials are endless in the winter of our souls, with short glimmers of hope that seem fleeting. A song called "Seasons of the Soul" by Michael and Stormie Omartian speaks to this feeling:

> Walkin' alone in the desert at night, searching for the rain,
>
> How can this happen to me it's not right, when Jesus is my friend,
>
> Everything was going fine,
>
> I was standing on the line,
>
> Where did I go wrong?
>
> Suddenly the sky was gray,
>
> Looking like it was gonna stay
>
> Far too long.
>
> Up on a mountain, I heard His sigh, like an angel's call,
>
> If you don't rest when the Winter is here, what will you bear in the Fall,
>
> A time to cry, a time to sing,
>
> There's a time for everything,
>
> Nothing lasts that long.
>
> Don't look at what you see,
>
> And just keep your eyes on Me,
>
> I won't let you go wrong.[2]

Winter is the in-between. It is the season of waiting. Waiting with expectation. Basking in the womb of time before birth happens. It is the transition point between what you were and what you are becoming. As you take advantage of the stillness and the darkness, understand that you are in preparation mode. You are being equipped inwardly for what will come to the surface shortly. Submit to the darkness and grow the muscles you need. Commit to fighting your way out of hindering mindsets and anything that

---

2. Michael and Stormie Omartian, "Seasons of the Soul," on *Seasons of the Soul* (Myrrh Records/MCA Records, 1978).

makes you feel bound. Stretch, feel the blood pumping through your veins. Unfold your wings, anticipate spring, and get ready to fly!

> *Brothers and sisters, we do not want you to be uninformed about those who sleep in death, so that you do not grieve like the rest of mankind, who have no hope.* (1 Thessalonians 4:13 NIV)

FOUR

GET OVER IT!

When life goes dark and you can't see the light at the end of the tunnel, it is easy to give up, roll over, and cease to function. Yet life continues around us. As winter gives way and yields to the brilliance of spring, so must our mourning over things that have been lost, relationships that have imploded, dreams that have dissipated, or long-held positions and even social stature that we no longer command. Whatever it is that you have held dear that is now gone, take the time to grieve—but don't get stuck there.

There are several reasons we get stuck in the mourning stage. When there is a sudden disruption or traumatic event, you can be blindsided and find it hard to find your footing. The lack of control over the situation, and the unexpectedness of it all, can lead you into various stages of grieving that can vary depending on the timeframe. Shock is the first stage, when you can't even locate a response because the reality of it all has yet to sink in. Some people choose to remain there, in denial, because to face the reality is just too painful.

When my boyfriend was killed years ago, he was laid to rest before I had the opportunity to see his dear, lifeless body. It left me perpetually in limbo. I comforted myself with the fact that because I had not seen him dead, he really wasn't gone. There were moments I thought I saw him across the street. My heart would race, and I would hasten my steps to see if it was really him. Of course, it wasn't him, and the day finally came when I had to accept that he was no longer on this earth.

Oh, the weeping and wailing and gnashing of teeth that had been put off way too long because I avoided the grieving process! I was told to be strong. People expected me to be instantly resilient. The truth of the matter was that I wasn't as strong as everyone had been led to believe. I was crumbling inside. My heart was shattered, and my mind was frayed around the edges. I felt I was losing it, and I entertained suicidal thoughts. But a strange mixture of pride and ego whispered to me that I needed to suck it up. *You cannot break!* it whispered. *What would people think? What would they say? How will you be viewed if you cannot cope?*

So I anesthetized myself. When the effects wore off, the pain was still there, leaving me to wrestle wordlessly against it. Until survival became a habit, and pain became my personal stalker, filling me with fear against an outburst that would make me look weak. I had just acquired the job of my dreams the same day he died, and I had to keep living. I. Had. To. Keep. Moving.

When life doesn't allow us to grieve, shed tears, acknowledge, and wallow in our pain for a time, we become emotional invalids paralyzed by our own cowardice. Yes, cowardice. Because at the end of the day, we are afraid to feel what we feel, not realizing we are feeling it in another way. Acting out in ways we fail to recognize as grieving. In the absence of embracing how we truly feel, we become a prisoner of our emotions or the lack thereof. Walls go up to shield us from further pain, but they also shut down our capacity to experience love and joy the way we should. It is quicksand at best. The more you fight against it, the more you get swallowed up by it.

But a phenomenal thing happens when we relax. The sand releases us, and we float to the surface. It no longer has a hold on us. A drowning man hastens his demise by flailing, but the moment he stops fighting and starts floating, he can make his way to safety—or at least hold on until someone rescues him.

Being able to relax and float on your pain will carry you to a safe place where you can take the time to reflect and put your pain in perspective. Dare to face and embrace your pain. Be strong enough to be weak. Yes, I said it. Let it fly. Scream. Cry. Throw something against the wall. Empty yourself. And wait for the refill. It's coming!

THE THINGS WE LOSE

When it comes to the death of a loved one, adjusting our thoughts on eternity can help us in the grieving process. When we can embrace that the separation is not final, just unwanted, we are able to make peace with the separation. When we embrace an eternal point of view that it is not the end of life but the transition to a greater life, we can actually rejoice that our loved one is in a better state.

Some may say that Jesus was harsh when He said, *"Let the dead bury their dead"* (Matthew 8:22 KJV). But He knew that what most people believed was a permanent condition was only temporary. That is why when His friend Lazarus died, He said, *"Our friend Lazarus has fallen asleep, but now I will go and wake him up"* (John 11:11). He knew it wasn't over for the deceased. As a matter of fact, it was just the beginning of true life!

The problem is we don't know about that life. We only know about the one we are living now without the person whom we love.

Sometimes the method of separation makes it harder to reconcile the experience. Violence, severe unending illness, and sudden, unexpected circumstances can jolt us seemingly beyond repair. Yet it is not the method of transition we should focus on because that is beyond our capacity to fix. It is the end of the matter. Whether that person suffered for a long time or a fleeting moment, the bottom line is that there is life beyond where we are. Not only that, but we will all die eventually. We will be reunited with those who went before us.

It's almost as if they took a trip to a fabulous place that you have always wanted to visit before you are able to get there. Since that is the reality, there should be a bit of envy and then joyful anticipation about going there yourself one day and seeing them again. It wouldn't matter that you couldn't talk every day anymore. You would sustain yourself with the great memories you built together and the fact that you know where they are, and you will be joyously reunited one day. To translate your grief into gratitude for the time spent together and the time to come is a way you can honor your loved ones.

There is a genuine fear of the unknown that wrestles with the question of why we die. And yet we will all transition to another place and life. When we have not settled this, it is because we fail to understand that every life has an expiration date, based on our purpose. When our assignment or purpose is completed, we leave and *graduate* to the next assignment. When our ability to be effective where we are is over, there is no need to remain. That is the compassion of God.

In other instances, the presence of sin in the world shortens the life of some without good reason. It makes no sense to us. We wrestle with why, and yet it is the consequence of being flawed in our humanity. We don't get to say how or when the best time is for anyone to leave, but we can decide that the relationship with them and the memory of them has instilled good in us that makes us conduct ourselves in a way that brings honor to them. Ask yourself how they would like you to live your life. If you could have that last conversation with them, what would they tell you about your life and your future? What state of heart and mind would they want you to adopt?

So much of how we are able to accept death is wrapped in our perception and acceptance of the reality of eternity. When we think of eternity fearfully rather than through the lens of faith, it creates great angst with projections of negativity and despair. We must remember that our emotions are derived from thoughts.

Therefore, your thoughts must be examined. Those things are feeding your paralysis and binding you to despair. The inability to move on and past the sadness must be dismantled so that it cannot rule over you. This requires discipline. The power you need to master your thought life and deny it permission to rule over your thoughts and attitudes resides inside your will. Replacing negatives with positives must become an exercise you utilize. After all, you are still here with a lot of living to do! How you live is up to you.

Another area where our grief can become debilitating can be found in false obligation. People have funny ideas about what will honor a person who has gone on before them. There is this morbid belief that professional mourning is honoring them. Remaining downcast and refusing to get over their departure is an obligation that no deceased loved one would ever desire for you. This is a twisted, false obligation that can keep you in a state of refusal or inability to recover. Sometimes it is attached to guilt. Grieving is penance for some, a way to fix the regrets of the past with that person. To fix the things that were said or done that shouldn't have been…or the things that should have been said or done but never were. This can keep you twirling in a perpetual struggle that will be difficult to resolve because there is no way to make amends except with yourself. In this case, you must forgive yourself. Release yourself. And know that in your imagination, the incident is probably magnified to be far greater than the actual occurrence.

THE POWER TO MOVE ON

Settling accounts with your heart and mind is critical to moving on.

I suffered severe guilt after the death of my boyfriend. We had argued. He had traveled. He got shot while on his trip. A friend of his said that if my boyfriend hadn't been angry, he wouldn't have traveled. It was all my fault!

These words echoed over and over in my soul as I spiraled downward into the abyss of my pain. My last conversation with him before this happened was not good. As he lay dying in a hospital across the country, I did not follow my instincts to go to him. His parents said he would need me more when he returned home, so I should just wait for him to come home. But he never returned home.

The scenarios that played out in my head were torturous. If I coulda, woulda, shoulda… But I couldn't, I wouldn't, and I didn't. Was it really my fault he was gone? No. He left a message with his family to console me because he anticipated my inability to handle his death, and yet I struggled to forgive myself for his demise.

It was only after I confessed that I accepted my imperfection in the relationship and became grateful for his love and God's forgiveness that I was able to break free and make peace with his departure. I took the time to be grateful for the moments we shared. The love and the laughter. I chose to preserve these thoughts as wonderful memories that would inform me that true love was possible, and I had experienced it. Finally, I was able to exhale and smile and love again.

Fact: Unrequited love, unfinished business, and unresolved issues can keep us in a state of perpetual regret. Yet you have the capacity to create resolution. Go ahead. Feel the emotion but put a time limit on how long you will live in your feelings because feelings are not accurate.

Focus on the truth. Focus on the options. Focus on having gratitude. Focus on new beginnings. Your feelings must follow your posture and decisions. Do not let them run amuck like a wayward child. Your decision to live whole and healthy is the adult that the child, your emotions, must obey.

Whether the loss you've suffered is a person or the death of a dream, business, career, or way of life, the same rules apply. It's never over. *There is always a next.* It's closer than you think, just beyond your despair. Hope and the faith that you can begin again are the first steps to the new life that awaits. Remember that life is an option filled with endless possibilities. So choose to keep living!

WHEN SHIFT HAPPENS

When life blindsides you with loss, whether it is expected or not, you must renew your vision and decide to begin again. Review your options for starting over and choose your path. What you anticipate will relegate how you move forward. You are more powerful than you know. The instinct to live even when you feel like dying is in your DNA. So take a deep breath and decide to defy your emotions. Command them to line up with your decision to not just survive, but to thrive, to come back better and stronger than before. Like the cedars of Lebanon, those trees known for their strength, let your breaking be your making.

MINDSHIFT

+ What thoughts are feeding your sadness? Are those thoughts true?

+ What mindsets need to shift to help you embrace gratitude?

+ What can you be grateful for as you consider your past and your future?

+ What are your options for moving forward?

+ What appointments will you make with yourself for recovery?

HINDSIGHT

A dead end is simply a vehicle put in place to redirect your focus and movement. The adage, "Time heals all things" seems trite, yet it is true. The reason we struggle with recovery is that we don't give ourselves permission to navigate through the process of healing. We will repeat every part we skip with greater difficulty. Accept that our experiences and losses never fade from our memory completely—they just move to a different place in our hearts, where we know how to find them in the right moments. This mindset releases us from the fear of permanent loss.

Ask yourself this question: What is the lesson learned or the diamond among the ashes that I can keep from my loss?

THE NEXT PRAYER

But one thing I do: Forgetting what is behind and straining toward what is ahead, I press on toward the goal to win the prize for which God has called me heavenward in Christ Jesus.

(Philippians 3:13–14 NIV)

Dear heavenly Father, I confess I have a tendency to hold onto things long after I should have let go. I have a hard time getting over the setbacks in my life. I don't know who I blame the most, those whom I deem guilty of disappointing and hurting me or myself for allowing it. I must admit I also blame You for not saving me from what I have suffered. I now realize the only prisoner in this instance is me. Help me to find the lesson in all of this, receive it, and let go. Help me to see my pain as a friend, revealing things I needed to know. Help me to make peace with the things I can't control. Help me to choose to trust You in the midst of my unanswered questions. Help me to see Your ultimate vision for me so that I press toward that goal rather than clinging to what has already occurred. Help me to see more hope in my future than in my present despair. Today I choose to forgive and let go. I choose to embrace the season that You offer and believe in greater things to come. I know You already saw what happened and prepared a solution. I am listening and will obey. Thank You for helping me through this difficult place. Thank You for the comfort that You offer. In the name of Christ Jesus. Amen.

What do you need to release?

_____

_____

_____

_____

What do you see ahead?

_____

_____

_____

_____

Write a faith confession here:

_____

_____

_____

_____

FIVE

LOCATE YOURSELF

This is a season where many are questioning their identity after experiencing losses of all kinds—physical, professional, relational, and financial. Are you questioning your relevance? Your abilities? Your future? Your capacity for impact? Your ability to thrive and succeed? Perhaps you are even questioning God for what He has allowed to occur in your life.

For many, who they are is tied to what they do and what they have. When those things are gone, they are at a loss regarding how to function or what direction to move in. Many who have been at the forefront of their fields eventually find themselves in a place of seeming obscurity and find it difficult to adjust to the lack of celebrity and high stature. It is a death of sorts. Who you are now is not who you were then. That was summer; this is winter. And yet the environment is the same.

The winter of our life can happen on different levels and in different sectors. Personal loss can occur not just in people or relationships. You can suffer economic loss. Positional loss. Professional loss. Loss of status.

Loss of health. Loss of mental acuity. Loss of finances. One often begets another, creating a domino effect of loss, a Job-like experience.

The biblical account of Job has modern-day significance when we look at it closely. It wasn't enough that Job lost his children. He lost property, assets, the respect of his wife, and his social standing. Once he had been touted as one of the wisest men in the land; now his friends gathered around not just to commiserate with him, but also to question his integrity and standing with God. (See Job 2:11–13; 15:4; 20:5.) They thought Job certainly must have done something wrong to bring all of this *bad luck* on himself. The reality of Job's life unraveling had not happened to them so they couldn't relate. Job's wife was no help at all. She told him, *"Are you still trying to maintain your integrity? Curse God and die"* (Job 2:9). Just give up, roll over, and don't even think about a comeback! In her mind, the events and losses that had occurred were beyond the hope of restoration.

Meanwhile, back at the ranch, Job sat in a state of disbelief as his mind grappled with all that had taken place. Trying to make sense of it all, he regretted the day he had been born (see Job 3:1–3) and made several sweeping statements that are continually quoted by others who have suffered various types of devastation. You know—things like, *"The* Lord *gave, and the* Lord *hath taken away; blessed be the name of the* Lord*"* (Job 1:21 kjv). Not exactly accurate, but it sounds good and poetic when one is trying to keep a brave face. But as time passed, either out of sheer exhaustion from being lectured and cross-examined by his friends or from hitting a wall as he tried to figure out why all of this had befallen him, Job admitted his undone state. His friends finally got everything off their chests as well.

WHEN THE TRUTH COMES OUT

One must wonder how long Job's friends had been thinking what they were thinking. Out of envy, were they reveling in the moment of finally feeling a bit of one-upmanship over Job? This is all sheer speculation, but it cannot be overlooked that Job's friends really expounded on all the areas where he may have gone wrong with great relish! It is at this point that God begins to speak and put everyone in their place and everything in perspective. The bottom line of His conversation points to His sovereignty and His ability to do as He pleases. Not out of cruelty, but to show Job and his friends that no matter what assaults you in life, there is always a *next*. He trusted Job to remain firmly entrenched in his faith throughout his trial and devastation, and he was rewarded and restored handsomely with double blessings in the end.

But let's backtrack a bit lest we lose the principle of the story. It wasn't just the physical loss that rocked Job. It was the internal issues at the very core of who he was, what he stood for, and what he believed that were at stake. For every accusation his friends hurled at him, Job stood firm in his convictions of who he was and what he believed about God. He did not bend or bow on these issues.

Trust me, someone will always have an opinion about your condition. They will have well-meaning advice, but you will have to weigh everyone's counsel and determine to separate fact from fiction. Some things are easier to figure out than others. In those moments when life seems fluid, you need to know you can master the flow. Who you are, what you stand for, and what you believe will have everything to do with the outcome of your situation. If you give in to negativity and believe the worse, this will become a self-fulfilling prophecy. If you resist the negative mindset to embrace the positive, you will make different confessions and different decisions that will bring you out of your predicament.

Job kept the faith even when the outward circumstances looked contrary to his beliefs. He said:

> My honor has blown away in the wind, and my prosperity has vanished like a cloud...So I looked for good, but evil came instead. I waited for the light, but darkness fell. My heart is troubled and restless. Days of suffering torment me. (Job 30:15, 26–27)

Yet after he said all of this, Job remained immovable in his convictions. He never questioned himself, his faith, or God. Usually, this is where self-doubt creeps in and we think, *Why me? What did I do wrong?* We get angry with God, wondering, *Why did He allow this to happen to me?* We may even become jealous or envious of others who seem to prosper while we suffer. All of these are distractions from where our focus should be.

MAKING A STAND

Job wouldn't budge on proclaiming his integrity. Neither did he flinch when he asserted that God was still very much alive and would come to his defense and decide the end of the matter for him. He believed in the *next* even though he didn't know what the next was! God finally showed up for Job after he passed the test of his heart. Then the Lord confronted Job's friends and told them He was offended because they had not spoken accurately about Him as Job had. (See Job 42:7.) To prove the accuracy of Job's expectations, He doubled Job's fortunes compared to what he had before. His latter days were greater than his former, he was more celebrated than before, and he even had seven more sons and three more daughters. (See Job 42:12–13.) And his friends gained a new and better understanding of God's character and His intentions toward those who serve Him. Even Job saw another side of God he didn't know before, noting, *"I had only heard about you before, but now I have seen you with my own eyes"* (Job 42:5).

What was the secret here? Job stayed focused on God's reputation though he mourned the loss of his own. He knew the source of everything he had, including his social standing.

Sometimes your shattered pride can be magnified even over your losses if you are married to your identity. Sometimes it's hard to believe that anything else is possible past your situation. Your pain, your loss, can overwhelm and saturate you until it becomes part of the fabric of who you are...if you let it. However, what happened to you is *not* who you are. It does not define you. To get stuck in this mindset is dangerous. It doesn't give you an out to move on. It shatters your hopes for a *next*.

We find another biblical story about someone who loses everything in the book of Ruth. Naomi is very much crippled by the events of her life, to the point where she embraces her broken identity.

Sometimes we miscalculate when to move and when to stay put. We are not our mistakes. Our losses do not define who we are or cause God to punish us. For everything we believe, say, or do, there is a consequence or a blessing. It is merely the outcome of choices. Different choices can correct bad choices if we don't bow to the present consequences.

No one would fault another for trying to make life better for themselves, especially when all the signs seem to point to the fact that a move should be made. That's what Naomi, her husband Elimelech, and their two sons did. The economy had tanked where they were, literally, and they perceived they were in a state of famine. The move was made to make a better life for their family. (See Ruth 1:1–2.) However, the place they chose was questionable. It's never a good time to make a decision when in a state of fear, anger, or pain. They settled in a land that was hostile to their values and beliefs. We don't know whose decision it was to move to a foreign land that would not support their faith or social mores. We don't even know if Naomi agreed with the move. All we know is that she went, and it cost her dearly. They left Judah or Canaan, which meant "land of the promise," to go to Moab, a land known for its false gods and sexual immorality. This is proof that desperation diminishes discernment, which leads us to make harmful choices to fix an issue we may not have a clear reading on.

How many of us settle for less than God's best when we misread the situation we are in or God's intentions toward us? When we don't understand His process, we tend to take life into our own hands. This usually doesn't end well.

WHEN LIFE HURTS

Naomi's husband died, which led to an even greater compromise in what was an already tenuous situation. Her sons married women from the region. Eventually, she was assaulted by overwhelming loss again when her sons died, leaving Naomi bereft with no options to consider where she was. She heard that everyone who had stayed put in Judah was prospering and things had returned to normal. She decided to return home. (See Ruth 1:6.)

This highlights my earlier point that our decisions should not be a knee-jerk reaction to a trial or be made in haste. Things are not always what they seem.

Those who faced the same losses as Naomi did back in Bethlehem—which meant "house of bread," speaking of provision—stayed where they were, weathered the storm, and experienced restoration with minimal losses. Naomi, on the other hand, lost what was more important than financial gain; she lost her family, her source of joy and hope. She also lost her sense of identity. Now that she was no longer a wife or a mother, who was she?

On the one hand, I commend her. She found the courage to cut her losses and return home. She did not allow pride to keep her from going back to face those she had left behind who were in a better position than she was. She obviously considered her options and chose the right one amid her grief. She only had two options at that point: stay and die, or move and live. She chose to live even though it is possible she didn't feel like it. Perhaps she thought if she must die, she'd rather die at home. We don't know the entire rationale behind her decision. She did have the presence of mind to tell her two daughters-in-law who decided to accompany her that there would be no future for them where she was heading. (See Ruth 1:11–13.) Just as she had come to an environment that was hostile to her spiritual values and social ethics, they would be going to an unwelcoming atmosphere where there would be no hope of them marrying again. One of them, Orpah, decided not to pursue change, to stick with what was familiar. The other, Ruth, decided to exercise her options and go with Naomi. *She was ready for her next.*

When we are broken, facing loss and devastation, our identity takes the biggest blow. When Naomi entered the city, those who knew her were excited to see her. They asked, *"Is it really Naomi?"* (Ruth 1:19). She told them to no longer call her *Naomi*, which means sweet or pleasant, but to call her *Mara*, which means bitter, *"for the Almighty has made life very bitter for me. I went away full, but the Lord has brought me home empty. Why call me Naomi when the Lord has caused me to suffer and the Almighty has sent such tragedy upon me?"* (Ruth 1:20–21).

Wait a minute. What did God have to do with it? Didn't she and her family leave because of perceived lack? Had God made life bitter for her… or did their own decisions result in the events leading up to her bitterness and sense of emptiness?

BEGINNING AGAIN

The first part of recovery from mistakes and losses is found in our ability to *own our stuff* so that we can assess not only how to move forward but what to avoid next time. Becoming bitter perverts our judgment and presents imaginary enemies into a scenario that can be easily explained as simply a wrong choice.

Don't beat yourself up about it. Your humanity gives you permission to make bad choices. Just don't stay there. Learn from them and make different choices. Pain can be your friend if utilized in a constructive, objective way. Let it teach you and equip you with wisdom. Now is not the time to blame others, yourself, or God.

Let us remember that God gives us free will and doesn't punish us for our choices. It is our choices that reward or correct us. Not God. There will be only one judgment at the end of time before the ultimate *next*—eternity.

Blame is a distraction from the lessons that could be learned and potential growth of character. Remember, for anyone you blame for an outcome you've experienced, you were also a participant. There is always something to be learned and an opportunity to empower you to discern and embrace your next.

Bitterness and blame are companions that can disable and paralyze you from moving forward. They can blind you from your next and convince you that life and your circumstances are hopeless. They distort your options through a deceptive smokescreen and magnify your weaknesses to shut you down. Remember this: no matter what you do or experience, you are still you. As they say, "One monkey don't stop no show!"

Fact: The attack on your mind will always be leveled at your identity and your self-worth. It is foundational to everything you do. What you know and believe about yourself will drive all your decisions. It will empower you and fuel your faith to move forward or disable you. It will also put into perspective what is truly important and sharpen your focus. It will separate fact from fiction. It will help you decide whether you stoop to a new low or realize you are bigger than whatever you face. More awaits as you decide to forcefully step into your next.

Both Job and Naomi had an identity crisis. They also both realized that life was not summed up by the face value of their circumstances but by something much deeper: faith in the One who identifies us no matter our state.

Your next will always ask you the question: Who are you? Your answer will determine your outcome.

I find it interesting that the tide changed for Naomi and Ruth when Naomi remembered who she was and what that meant. She was connected to a powerful family and a man who could redeem them from their situation. As she instructed Ruth on how to tap into her familial rights, her position shifted. (See Ruth 2:19–22.) Naomi went out full and returned empty to a happy ending that reads like something out of a fairytale, and yet it was very true. Her restoration went beyond her wildest dreams as Ruth wed the kind and wealthy Boaz and gave birth to a child who would become the grandfather of David, king of Israel—who also happened to be in the lineage of Christ, by the way! (See Ruth:4:13.)

> *Then the women of the town said to Naomi, "Praise the* Lord, *who has now provided a redeemer for your family! May this child be famous in Israel. May he restore your youth and care for you in your old age. For he is the son of your daughter-in-law who loves you and has been better to you than seven sons!" Naomi took the baby and cuddled him to her breast. And she cared for him as if he were her own. The neighbor women said, "Now at last Naomi has a son again!"* (Ruth 4:14–17)

Naomi's life, her joy, and her identity were restored by pouring herself into someone else. Sometimes our identity is not found in what we accomplish but by the legacy of those we love and help. This is the ultimate restoration and fulfillment.

WHEN SHIFT HAPPENS

Amid crisis, don't lose your bearings by forgetting who you are. It's important to have a plan and have options. Don't get thrown off track by deviations; see them as opportunities to redirect your path and get better traction. More than often, delay comes disguised as death. Stay clear on what you are facing.

MINDSHIFT

+ Who are you?

+ What has happened? How has this affected your sense of identity?

+ Where is the opportunity in this?

+ What lie are you tempted to believe? What is the truth of your situation?

+ What are your options for restoration?

HINDSIGHT

It's all right to give yourself permission to mourn over the person that you *were*. However, now is the time to discover the person that you *can be*—an even greater you. Don't beat yourself up over any decisions you made in the past. Recognize that the things you did then served you in that season, take the lessons forward, and stay open to changes.

Ask yourself this question: What did you learn in the latter season that can serve you in this season to become a better, more fruitful person?

THE NEXT PRAYER

The Lord's light penetrates the human spirit, exposing every hidden motive.   (Proverbs 20:27)

Dear heavenly Father, sometimes I am not aware of my own heart condition. Why I do what I do escapes me. Only You can reveal the hidden motives of my heart and help me to embrace truth like a friend. I realize I need to be honest with myself and with You to get the help I need. Help me to welcome the truth rather than fear it. Help me not to avoid my own reflection, but to look into Your eyes and see what You see. Help me to be willing to dig deep so that I can uproot the things in me that hinder my progress and keep me from experiencing the breakthrough I long for. I realize my greatest hindrance is myself. I want to renew my mind so that my life can be transformed. Speak Your words of truth to me, Lord. I receive the clarity You bring, in the name of Christ Jesus. Amen.

What truth do you need to face about yourself?

_____

_____

_____

_____

How will acknowledging the truth help you move forward?

_____

_____

_____

_____

Write a faith confession here:

_____

_____

_____

_____

SIX

MAKE THAT MOVE

Have you been ejected from your comfort zone in a way that has upset your equilibrium? Have you been an involuntary victim of sudden change that was out of your control? Have you felt a sense of urgency to make changes in your life due to unsustainable circumstances? Are you living under a cloud of regret for making the wrong choice? Are you second-guessing the move you made? Are you reluctant to accept change? Feeling paralyzed and overwhelmed as things shift around you? Good news! You are not alone.

People respond to change differently. Some are willing to take the leap, feeling any move is better than no move at all. Some see change as a chance for a new beginning. Still others linger on the past even if the past was not desirable. Not everyone is comfortable with change, yet if you wait long enough, life will force you to make moves you otherwise would not have made voluntarily.

In my own life, struggling to rebound after the attacks of September 11, 2001, mismanagement in my office caused my ministry calendar to go blank and my finances to dry up. I was able to rebound and begin again.

New staff and a new book got me back on my feet. And just when I thought I was back on a good roll, it happened: A series of closed doors. Financial loss that led to the foreclosure of my home. Returning my office back to the bank. The death of my father. Like dominoes tumbling in succession, life seemed to be falling all around me. This time, there was no speedy recovery. I couldn't figure it out, and no one could give me a good explanation for what was happening—or, better yet, not happening. Another lesson: the same solution doesn't always work in the same circumstances. Being open to new options is critical to your progress and your ability to overcome difficulty. I spread my hands out before God and said, "Lord, what am I supposed to do?" I heard the words, "Move to Ghana!" What?! That wasn't on my retirement list, want-to list, or bucket list. No list I had. Yet I felt compelled. As compelled as the Israelites, who after initially resisting the leadership of Moses, got sick of the plagues in Egypt and were ready to leave when he said "go."

I will admit I might not have been so inclined if my circumstances had been different. If I was still running full throttle and in demand, I might have had several excuses for negotiating with God on such a drastic move. What was I going to do in Ghana anyway? I always enjoyed my visits there during holidays with my father, but living there permanently had never entered my mind. And yet I followed where God pointed. It was definitely an Abraham move. I didn't know what lay ahead; I simply moved in faith.

Have I regretted it? Absolutely not. Did I expect to find my dreams fulfilled there? Not on your life. Yet I would say that God has a capricious sense of humor, a *double-dog-dare-you-to-try-Me* kind of humor that flies in the face of our intellect to prove His sovereignty and His ability to cause us to thrive despite ourselves.

THE POWER OF OBEDIENCE

Three weeks after sensing this direction, all of my worldly goods were on a container floating across the ocean while I was on a plane with my three Shih Tzu fur babies, headed to Ghana. Although I visit the United States often, I've never looked back in the sense of wanting to live there again. Several of my dreams have come true in Ghana. I discovered things about myself, stretching and growing in ways I would never have expected.

I am richer for the experience. I have cultivated new skills that have heightened my ability to have a positive impact on the lives of many in several unorthodox ways. Things that had been dormant in me were brought back to new life, giving me tremendous fulfillment. Who knew anything good could come out of all those losses that seemed so devastating at the time? I admit I did not. But apparently, God did!

I believe there are many just like myself who find themselves between a rock and a hard place. Sometimes the box we find ourselves in is our own minds, but sometimes, life paints us into a corner. We see no way out. It's hard to imagine other options beyond our familiar ones. It literally takes blind faith to take the leap and trust goodness to catch us.

As we noted in the last chapter, Ruth, Naomi's daughter-in-law, did not know what her next step would be. After the death of her husband, father-in-law, and brother-in-law, she chose to take a gamble based on what she *did* know: the relationship she had with her mother-in-law. When Naomi decided to leave Moab and return to Bethlehem, Ruth decided to accompany her. Orpah, her sister-in-law, upon the revelation that there would be no husbands for them where Naomi was going, decided to stay behind in Moab. When you seek to save your life, you lose it. We don't hear anything else about Orpah; she vanished into obscurity. Ruth, however, would not be deterred. She decided where they were living no longer served her. Instead, her future would be determined by the relationship she kept with Naomi, Naomi's people, and their God, as well as where she positioned herself. Ruth was not bitter over her losses; she was open to the endless possibilities no matter how hopeless Naomi painted the scenario. She believed there was something beyond where she presently stood, and she was willing to put the past behind her and go for it.

Though she knew her people, the Moabites, were considered enemies of the Israelites, Ruth trusted that her character and wisdom would speak louder than her identity, and she chose to move, not just physically but spiritually. She let go of everything familiar, and the rest is history. She went from being an *enemy* in a society that was hostile to her people to becoming the revered great-grandmother of David, the king of Israel, and entering the lineage of Christ. One move was not only a step out of loss but a step into a phenomenal legacy.

Who knows what awaits you when you decide to step into your next? Sometimes the way does not reveal itself until you take the first step, then another and another. Like Harrison Ford's character in *Raiders of the Lost Ark*,[3] sometimes the thing you need to support your steps won't appear until you take a step of faith.

THE FUTURE AWAITS

I had no idea what I would do once I got to Ghana besides a few obvious things that were in place. As time went on, the reason I thought I was moving disappeared, and new opportunities I had only dreamed of in the past presented themselves to me!

Some things cannot be figured out ahead of time. You must dare to step out! When life hems you in and there appear to be no options, you must believe there is still a next! Take the time to quiet your soul, listen to the still small voice within prompting you to walk toward what may not be obvious, and trust God to direct you and sustain you as you follow where His finger points. Peace will be your confirmation even as others may not agree with your path.

I have to tell you, my friends thought I was nuts when I announced I was moving. But I knew deep in my soul that it was the thing to do. I pressed past the resistance and, as the saying goes, others understood it *by and by*—but initially, it was a hard sell.

Small wonder that Orpah, Ruth's sister-in-law, went back home. Her faith was not on the same level as Ruth's. Also, her focus was different. She was all right with what was familiar to her. And, obviously, marrying again was on the top of her priority list since she was told there would be no prospects where she was going.

Ruth wanted more. She wanted a new life, a new God, and new experiences. She had been there, done that, in Moab. She was up for the adventure. She also had a committed relationship with Naomi.

You never know where your relationships and alignments will take you. Community is important. Relationships and support systems are

---

3. *Raiders of the Lost Ark*, directed by Steven Spielberg (1982; Paramount Pictures).

important. Geography is also important. Those closest to you will have a massive effect on where you find yourself.

Naomi and Ruth seemed to have an unusually close relationship, so close that Ruth chose to forsake her comfort zone to step into the unknown and accompany her mother-in-law to a place that did not look promising! Yet she was willing to take the risk. Destiny was waiting for her on the other side.

Your next is waiting for you too.

Fact: They say necessity is the mother of invention, but I believe it is also the catalyst for change. Until the pain of staying the same is greater than the pain of change, you won't change. Yes, even when change is desired, it can initially be painful. And frightening. It requires pressing past your reservations, not needing to have the answer to every question. It demands that you corral your imagination, separating fact from fiction and forming a strategy to the best of your ability based on the amount of information you presently have. That's why it is called the *walk of faith.* Walking by faith can be a great adventure. It depends on how you look at those moments when you will be compelled to launch into the unknown.

I think of another daring woman in the Bible, a prostitute and innkeeper named Rahab. Tired of her life and knowing that Israel was going to attack her city of Jericho, she saw no way out.

What do you do when you feel stuck? When you lack the support that you need to make a change? What if your way of life is all you know…yet there is this desire burning inside of you for something else, something more?

TAKING THE RISK

Rahab was able to discern a window of opportunity. One day, two strangers showed up at her door—foreigners who were planning a hostile takeover of her city! While others all over Jericho quaked in fear over their impending doom, Rahab looked past the present to see how the situation could serve her. (See Joshua 2:4–14.) She chose to be a victor rather than a victim. She looked for the escape route out of the disastrous end. She took a risk. She formed a new alliance. Her relationship with those two

Israelite spies had everything to do with her next. She would help them escape if they would agree to help her and her family escape annihilation. This was admirable, as it was a time when the first instinct would normally be self-preservation—every man or woman for themselves.

But Rahab, someone whose work did not reflect a commitment to relationships, was more committed than most. Perhaps because of her work, she felt isolated and therefore treasured her support system more. Who knows? She probably helped support her family with her income. She was a high-class call girl with a powerful and wealthy clientele. It was clear that her clients were top level—politicians, people in high places. Her house was right in the outer wall of the city. She was known to the king of Jericho. (See Joshua 2:3.) The money was good, but life was not. Now was the time for her to grasp the opportunity to tap into her next.

While Solomon said, *"A party gives laughter, wine gives happiness, and money gives everything!"* (Ecclesiastes 10:19), Rahab knew you can't purchase peace. Her way of life left her with a void in her soul that no material gain could fill. She saw the opportunity for a new beginning and literally took a leap of faith even though it put her life at stake. She took the risk of defying the king and his officials to hide the spies and help them escape. Perhaps she had come to realize that she was merely existing and that wasn't the life she wanted. With her heart in her throat, she evaded the questions of those who came looking for the spies. She realized this was a matter of life and death. She decided to give her life away to save it. And what a life it was.

After the city was taken, Rahab and her family were rescued, just as the spies had promised. (See Joshua 6:22–23.) That was the beginning of an entirely new life—a life where she would marry a man named Salmon and have a son named Boaz. Boaz would also marry a foreigner, and they would become the great-grandparents of David, the king of Israel. Who would have ever dreamed that this would be the end of a story that began with no hope? Did Rahab imagine that her next would be so glorious? I don't believe she did.

When we dare to take a step of faith, God will always meet us on the other side. The phrase "above and beyond what you could imagine" comes to mind. We always think smaller than the real possibilities. The difference between those who dream and those whose dreams come true is action: doing something that propels you beyond what you wish for.

When we think of people like Elon Musk, Steve Jobs, or Mark Zuckerberg, or biblical characters like Abraham and Noah, the word *risk-taker* comes to mind. In the face of skepticism or lack of reference, these people dared to dream of very different tomorrows and take steps to implement what they envisioned despite opposition, resistance, or even the greater element of moving toward the unknown. Yet their lives and accomplishments speak for themselves. They have made their mark in society and have cemented life-changing legacies that have affected the masses. The difference between them and you is being willing to take a risk, believing in what you dream.

Rahab weighed her options—nothing...or something new. She didn't know what that something was, but it was better than nothing.

Whether you are adventurous or not, breaking from the old to embrace change in your life requires courage and passion. When you reach the point where you have nothing to lose, rejoice because this is when you will find you have everything to gain. When your back is against the wall literally, and there seems to be no other choice, get excited. Your next is near!

WHEN SHIFT HAPPENS

When you get sick and tired of being sick and tired, it can lead to a place of resignation and apathy that inhibits your resolve and drains you of the energy needed to break out of your circumstances. It is that one last push a pregnant woman must do to be able to birth new life.

MINDSHIFT

+ What needs to happen to get you to move?

+ What fears do you harbor about moving forward? Are they true?

+ What are your options?

+ What do you really want?

+ What do you need to do to achieve what you want?

HINDSIGHT

Very few people step into change readily. The catalyst for change is usually preceded by upheaval, pain, anger, or lack. Our emotions can paralyze us or champion us. It is important to examine how you feel about where you are and define what that means. Be honest with yourself about your vulnerabilities and your abilities. Weigh your options and enlist help to formulate a plan.

Ask yourself this question: What is really holding you back from making the move you need to make? What would happen if things remained the same?

THE NEXT PRAYER

I press toward the mark for the prize of the high calling of God in Christ Jesus. (Philippians 3:14 KJV)

Dear heavenly Father, to move from where I am will take supernatural strength. I feel so rooted to the spot where I am right now. I feel I am unable to move forward. The wind has been knocked out of my sails and I am laboring to keep breathing. I know that with Your help, I can overcome how I feel right now. As I choose to walk by faith and not by sight, help me recover the strength I need to gain the momentum I need to move forward past this place I am in. Help me to develop blinders that see only what awaits me. Help me to blot out every distraction, including my past and my pain. Restore the joy of living to me. Help me not to grow bitter but better. Revive me and help me to see the light at the end of the tunnel and run toward it. I know that there is more waiting for me. Yet my faith wavers in the light of where I am at present. Help my unbelief in the name of Christ Jesus. Amen.

What is robbing you of your joy and strength?

_____

_____

_____

_____

Where should your focus be at this time?

_____

_____

_____

_____

Write a faith confession here:

_____

_____

_____

_____

SPRING

The first bloom of hope—the budding of flowers, birds singing—is the heralding of new life, new beginnings, and a fresh start. Even the air smells different. It is the time of renewal, rebirth, rejuvenation, and regrowth. To the Christian, it signifies the season of the resurrection.

To many, the spiritual meaning of spring is significant: it is a time of fertility, a season of birthing. Now you begin to see the glimmers of hope and a new season in your life. The days are longer, the sun is brilliant and warming, and the fresh breezes blend the heady scent of blossoming plants and trees. You can smell a literal revival of all that died in the winter. Those gray days are behind us, and the golden rays of spring give us new energy, new ideas, and renewed faith.

Yes, God makes all things new. He is faithful to give us a reprieve from the trials and challenges of life. A time to catch our breath, to gain strength to continue. Literally, spring is the comma between the seasons of our lives, the rest in the middle of the song that revives us to continue the dance of life. It gives us a glimpse of things to come.

Easter is appropriately celebrated in the spring, commemorating the resurrection of Jesus Christ. We proclaim, "He has risen—He is risen indeed." And so have our dreams, our hopes, and the desires we've harbored. As nature died, so did He, and both have come back to life, suggesting that death is not permanent but transitory. It's never *really* over. We go from life to life to life!

Just as a seed must die to produce fruit, our dreams die for a season. In the spiritual cycle, the dream dies three times before it is realized. As the root of what we long for and dream about burrows deeper and deeper into our hearts, it finds a firm foundation to attach itself to. The higher and weightier the dream, the deeper the root must travel, and the longer it takes to burst to the surface. But, oh, when it is time, nothing can stop it from bearing glorious fruit that feeds many!

Any dream worth having will bless many others besides you. Therefore, it needs to be firmly rooted in order to withstand the pulls of others grasping at what you have to offer. Without deep roots, major acquisitions, fame, and promotion will always set you up for disaster.

Our character lies in our roots; it is what we are when no one is watching, waiting to be revealed when we have an audience.

Though it looks as if nothing is happening in winter, you can rest assured that a lot is going on beneath the surface, and spring is coming in all its glory, revealing the growth done in secret.

Literally, the atmosphere changes. The silence of winter gives way to sounds of celebration from nature and humanity. People get a bit more pep in their step. Activities begin to accelerate. As bears and other animals come out of hibernation, so do people. Those who traveled to warmer climates to escape the cold return. Some animals change color to blend in with their habitats for safety. Farmers plant their seeds for summer crops. Rain falls, seemingly washing the earth, giving her a pristine finish while watering the seeds that have been sown.

In some cases, spring heralds a time of drastic weather changes and storms that wash away anything that is not firmly rooted in place, leaving the victims devastated and forced to start over again in the face of losses.

And yet for most, it is a time of festivity. Coats come off. Colors are revealed. Everything is vibrant and alive. The atmosphere changes. People feel invigorated. New projects are launched. Love is in the air. Romance is in bloom. There is an enthusiastic expectation of better tomorrows. It's all about hope. It springs eternal, pardon the pun.

The late comedian Robin Williams said, "Spring is nature's way of saying, 'Let's party!'"

I think most of us have something wonderful to say about spring. The prophet Zechariah wrote:

Ask the LORD for rain in the spring, for he makes the storm clouds. And he will send showers of rain so every field becomes a lush pasture.

(Zechariah 10:1)

As you consider your own life, breathe in the scent of new beginnings. Those latent dreams and past disappointments are compost for the seeds that have been planted in your heart. Every season has an expiration date. In the fullness of time, the appointed time, this too will come to pass. A new life awaits. Harvest will come; it is inevitable if you keep planting, watering, nurturing, and waiting for it. Understanding the season and its purpose is critical. If you watch closely, you will begin to see the ground shifting making way for fruitfulness. Just be aware that as your dreams are realized, there will still be a next!

Assess where you are now and gain clarity:

+   What season are you in? What is the purpose of your season?

+   What seeds have you planted? How have you prepared for harvest?

+   What have you learned about yourself while waiting for your desire to come to fruition?

+   What needs to shift in your mindset to accommodate your vision?

Spring is the preamble of summer when the fullness of everything you've worked and hoped for come to the fore. That season has its own issues. It must be noted that some flowers that beautify the landscape in the spring, such as tulips, don't last in the summer. I once attended the Tulip Festival in Holland, Michigan, where the brilliance of the flowers and their beauty was a sight to behold. But alas, tulips don't have the capacity or the constitution to last through the summer, so other things are planted to take their place.

We need to know not just the seasons, but also who and what are seasonal elements in our lives. Not all things are designed to last for a lifetime; some only last for a season. When we understand this, we gain the capacity to let go of people and things with gratitude and joy because their departure creates room for our next. No matter how we look at it, there is always a next.

*See, the former **things** have taken place, and **new things** I declare; before they spring into being I announce them to you.*

(Isaiah 42:9 NIV)

SEVEN

KEEP LOOKING UP

Distraction is one of the greatest deterrents holding us back from reaching our next. The beautiful thing about nature is that the earth is well aware of what needs to take place at specific times in order to complete the mission of that season. Spring is all about birthing new things, production, fruitfulness, and taking life to the next level. The characteristics of the season do not change. Even when there are drastic changes in the weather, the seasons continue. It still snows in winter, the leaves still turn in fall, and flowers still bloom in spring. In the tropics, it still rains during the rainy season. The cycle of life spurs each season on to the next movement.

Fruitfulness demands growth, painful pruning, and then regrowth. Trials, challenges, and yes, even the death of certain things in our lives should increase us not deplete us. Pruning looks painful and ugly, but it makes way for richer, lusher, sweeter fruit! This is where we dig deeper, fight to survive, and flourish as we keep our focus on the sun, the promise of better days and the fulfillment of dreams and dormant desires. Every flower, every tree, strains to face the sun. Even after the rain, their posture is that of looking up. In particular, sunflowers face east to catch the sun at its rising in the springtime, and their heads move to catch its rays throughout the day.

Fact: Nature does not bow to the elements; plants grow despite them. They return full force, producing richer and greater fruit in response to being purged either by the hand of the gardener or adversity.

What is your posture when change or calamity is thrust upon you? Do you fold within yourself? Do you look down? Look up? Look around? Become easily distracted and thrown off course? Where is your focus? What do you believe when things shift off course in your life? Are you still able to maintain the big picture in your line of sight? Are you still able to visualize where you were headed and see what you want in front of you? Are you thrown off track, or are you able to bounce back?

Resilience is needed in times of critical change. I believe the secret to this is not to cling too tightly to anything. Being able to wear life loosely provides room for changes and repositioning without trauma. If you are riding on a bus that suddenly stops, you are likely to tumble if your knees are rigid but if your stance is relaxed, you will bounce back. That's how you should approach life so that you will still be standing if circumstances attempt to throw you.

When we build up a dependency on something, we feel a great sense of loss as well as being lost when it's gone. But life goes on around you. As long as you are here, you are still filled with purpose. Your *next* and your destiny awaits you on the other side of your disruption.

DISCERNING THE TIMES

Elijah was a mighty prophet with a promising mentee, Elisha, among his other students. When he sensed it was his time to go, Elijah set out, following God's leading, and told Elisha to remain behind. But Elisha perceived what was about to occur and refused to leave his mentor's side. (See 2 Kings 2:1–7.) Three times, Elijah tried to dissuade Elisha from accompanying him, but he refused to go away or be diverted from his course.

Others chimed in from the company of the prophets to distract Elisha, asking him, *"Did you know that the LORD is going to take your master away from you today?* (verse 5). Elisha's response was a healthy, *"Of course I know…But be quiet about it."*

Elijah told Elisha, *"Stay here, for the* L<small>ORD</small> *has told me to go…"* first to Jericho, then to Bethel, and then finally to the Jordan River (2 Kings 2:2, 4, 6). Each time, Elisha replied, *"As surely as the* L<small>ORD</small> *lives and you yourself live, I will not leave you."*

Why am I telling you this story? Because the principles for transition into a new season, your personal spring, are so clear.

First, have a vision of where you are going and what you want. Elijah knew his time was up and it was time to pass the baton. Elisha wanted a double portion of Elijah's anointing and was determined to follow him until he got it. (See 2 Kings 2:9.) He was given the opportunity to turn back three times. Twice, people showed up to distract Elisha from his mission. (See 2 Kings 2:3, 5.) There will be those who show up to ask why you are persisting in your mission. This usually increases the closer you get to your goal. Everyone is happy to sit and commiserate with you in your winter when it seems like nothing is happening because nothing is happening for them either. Of course, misery loves company.

Those who laid around the pool of Bethesda for years with no hope of recovery supported one another's stagnation. It took Jesus coming along and disrupting the mindset of one invalid who had been lying there for thirty-eight years to get him to stand up and walk. (See John 5:2–9.) He didn't know it was possible until someone broke through the voices that kept validating the thoughts that life would always be more of the same, being broken and paralyzed. But everything changed in a moment when a divine disruption occurred.

Your environment and your support system have everything to do with your ability to flourish. Yes, the closer you get to spring, the louder the voices of doubt and questioning will become. But keep looking up. Keep your eye on the prize. Spring is coming! If you are on the right track, the last blasts of cold wind disguised in the form of naysaying and questioning will come, but you must shake off doubts and distraction—just like Jesus who for the joy that was set before Him endured the journey and did not allow Himself to be distracted or pulled off course from His mission. (See Hebrews 12:2.) Yes! Focus is required.

Fact: Distractions will always exist. Completing what you've started is optional but it's within your power to do so. All it takes is a decision.

While the company of prophets gathered to question why Elisha was still following Elijah, Elisha remained focused. Elijah had told Elisha that if he saw him when he got caught up into heaven, he would be able to acquire a double portion of his anointing. (See 2 Kings 2:9–10.)

What is the principle here? You can have what you see, what you envision, and what is real to you! Your body and your actions will follow your focus. If change is what you are after, if another level of living is what you want, or if you are longing for a new beginning, you must focus without giving into distraction. Doublemindedness will get you nowhere. Second-guessing yourself will stop you in your tracks and hinder your progress. Keep. Looking. Up.

STAYING ON COURSE

Despite the voices that could have caused him to give up his quest and consider his pursuit hopeless, Elisha kept his eyes on the prize. And he got it. He saw *"a chariot of fire…drawn by horses of fire…and Elijah was carried by a whirlwind into heaven"* (2 Kings 2:11). Elisha captured the moment in his mind and his heart; the truth that elevation was possible resonated in his soul. He saw his next in clear view. He caught Elijah's cloak and got the anointing he wanted. He went from winter to spring at that moment. Promotion came swiftly.

Yes, spring is appropriately named. It springs upon us. After waiting for the climate of our lives to change, we go from a blank canvas to a myriad of beautiful activities. The difference between the soil and us is that the soil lies in expectation of spring and is fully ready to receive the newness of life that comes with it. Flowers are prepared to fight for the right to blossom. Something is built into their DNA that makes them push through the dirt, grow, and show up in all their glory. After being beaten by spring showers and even more severe storms that may cause them to lose their initial petals, they are bowed but not broken. They blossom again with an even more magnificent crown.

What about you? It is also in your DNA, spiritually and physically, to push through the mess. It is the compost, that same mess that fertilizes our ideas and the desires of our hearts to grow despite the rain and the storms that can challenge and assault us. At times, it may seem that you've lost your former glory, your capacity to flourish and shine, but something inside you refuses to give up. Follow that. Stretch. Scream. Even rest a while, but make sure you pull yourself out of your bowed over position, straighten yourself, and purpose to thrive and flourish. You were made for this, and you cannot deny what has been placed inside of you by the One who lovingly created you! He knew what you would encounter at every turn and every season, and He equipped you for the journey. So don't get distracted. Focus and follow through.

To get to the promised land, the Israelites had to follow a cloud by day and a pillar of fire by night. (See Exodus 13:21.) They had to keep looking up to reach their next. When Peter looked down while walking on water to reach Jesus, he began to sink and almost drowned. (See Matthew 14:28–31.) A fisherman who was used to storms and knew how to swim became overwhelmed by something stronger than his knowledge and experience. Fear almost wiped him out because he failed to keep looking up.

GROWING PAINS

As the flowers turn their face to the sun, reaching to the sky, they are promoted to growth and glory. Spring is the season of growth. All growth is not comfortable. Some things must fall off to make room for the greater. Purging takes place.

You need to reject the things and people who appear to be acceptable but in truth are stunting your growth and hindering your capacity to produce greater fruit. Stretching beyond the limitations you've grown used to and the familiar can sometimes make you fearful. Take your eyes off your limited abilities and internal questions that do not serve you. By faith, keep looking up, keeping your dream in sight.

Looking up is not just a figurative phrase. It describes a state of mind. It speaks of optimism and expectancy. Looking up is not just about physical posture. It is spiritual and mental. Looking up is having a posture of faith, believing in the endless possibilities that await you in every area of your life. Looking up is a posture that demands you follow through with positive action no matter what anyone says, how you may feel, or even what your eyes tell you at the moment. It is having the vision to see beyond where you are to where you want to be. It is calling those things that are not as though they were, utilizing the creative power of your heavenly Father to speak things that He has placed in your heart into existence. (See Romans 4:17.) Your actions will follow your speech, creating the conditions that will make you see your vision realized. It is setting your sights on higher ground—such as that promotion, that breakthrough, that better relationship, or that state of financial abundance that frees you to generously give to others while experiencing security.

It is possible. It is in view, but you must go through the process to reach it. You've got to be determined enough to push through the unbroken ground. You've got to endure the rain and the storms. Don't let these things dissuade you from blooming, blossoming, and flourishing! Look up! The sun is shining, and it's calling you to your next!

WHEN SHIFT HAPPENS

When you've weathered through a season of sameness and the calm is shattered by disruption, it's time to get excited. It is the birthing season. A woman in labor wants to give up before that last push, but that is the time to bear down. The same is true for you. Break through the soil. Stretch. Grow. Be open to new life. Embrace your new beginning. This is the next you've been waiting for!

MINDSHIFT

+ What barriers do you feel you need to break through?
+ What do you feel has been stopping you before?
+ What do you need to focus on currently?
+ How do you need to follow through?
+ How have you grown during this time?

HINDSIGHT

Barriers and storms are not a *no*, but devices that God uses to help you develop muscles to sustain your next. Embrace the lessons. Revel in the process and reap the reward. Ask yourself this question: What other option do you have if you don't follow through on your dream?

THE NEXT PRAYER

[Looking away from all that will distract us and] focusing our eyes on Jesus, who is the Author and Perfecter of faith [the first incentive for our belief and the One who brings our faith to maturity], who for the joy [of accomplishing the goal] set before Him endured the cross, disregarding the shame, and sat down at the right hand of the throne of God [revealing His deity, His authority, and the completion of His work].

(Hebrews 12:2 AMP)

Dear heavenly Father, I am far too distracted by what is going on. I have lost sight of my end goal. Restore my vision and give me a second wind. As I consider what is before me, let it be the incentive I need to shake off all that keeps me bound and discouraged. Help me to cast off all that does not matter to focus on that which is lasting and of great importance. Empower me with the faith I need in this season to keep my eyes on You rather than my circumstances. Help me to complete what I have started and accomplish my goals. Help me to press past disillusionment and procrastination to complete the vision You have given me in excellence, in the name of Christ Jesus. Amen.

What are your present distractions?

_____

_____

_____

_____

What do you need to focus on right now?

_____

_____

_____

_____

Write your faith confession here:

_____

_____

_____

_____

EIGHT

FORGET ABOUT IT!

Once upon a time, there was a woman who lived in a society that was deteriorating at a rapid rate. (See Genesis 19:1–22.) She, her husband Lot, and their two daughters were foreigners who had assimilated into the present culture, but they were still regarded as outsiders. Their daughters were engaged to men in this new territory; the family had relaxed their ethics, religious beliefs, and morality as they embraced the norms there. Two strangers came to town and warned them of the city's impending doom. They told Lot that he and his family had to leave immediately. There was no time for delay. The two daughters' fiancés poo-pooed the whole idea, laughing it off and choosing to remain behind. Literally grabbing Lot and his family by the hands and escorting them out of the city, the strange visitors told them, "Whatever you do, don't look back!" Lot agreed to this, and with his wife and two daughters in tow, fled as fire and brimstone began to fall upon Sodom.

Who knows what thoughts were running through the mind of Lot's wife when all of this happened? Was she thinking of things she was leaving behind? Worrying about the welfare of a friend she didn't have the chance to say goodbye to? Feeling conflicted about the move being made in so much haste? We don't know. All we know is that she did the unspeakable—she looked back. At that moment, before she could correct her position and continue forward, she turned into a pillar of salt and was left behind, rooted to the spot.

Why salt, I wonder? Salt is actually supposed to be a good thing. It's used for flavoring and preserving food. It balances fluids in the blood and maintains healthy blood pressure. It's also used for tanning, dyeing, bleaching, and a number of other things. Yet too much salt can make food inedible. It can also contribute to cardiovascular disease, fluid retention, kidney problems, osteoporosis, heart failure, and stroke.

In the case of Lot's wife, it was immobilizing. While her family moved hastily away from the destruction at hand, girlfriend wasn't going anywhere. She was stuck. This was her heart condition that manifested in the physical. She couldn't go back, but she also could not move forward.

How many have found themselves in this same space? Filled with so many regrets, doubts, fears, and questions that it hindered any progress they could and should be experiencing?

LOOKING BACK

There are times when the past gets way too much credit as we romanticize the very things we hated while we wished for a new life. Like the Israelites who longed for the foods they ate in Egypt while they were in the wilderness on their way to the promise land.

> *"Oh, for some meat!" they exclaimed. "We remember the fish we used to eat for free in Egypt. And we had all the cucumbers, melons, leeks, onions, and garlic we wanted. But now our appetites are gone. All we ever see is this manna!"* (Numbers 11:4–6)

They romanticized the food of slavery, food they'd eaten while they were held captive in Egypt. They might have hated the leeks and onions, but they hated the uncertainty of their next even more. In the middle of the desert—not knowing what to expect, not really trusting God's promise of a land flowing with milk and honey—they reminisced about things and times that once grieved them. They whined, complained, and desired to return to the very things they cried out to God to deliver them from. They could only see the past; they could not look beyond to the possibilities beckoning them toward a new life of freedom and abundance. This mentality was deeply rooted in their subconscious. I suspect they were totally unaware of why they resisted change so much. They were out of Egypt, but Egypt was still in them.

After years of being slaves, being free was a foreign concept too good to be true! Was it really possible? If so, what was taking so long? Wasn't it supposed to be a much shorter journey? Why did they have to wander through the wilderness and cross rivers? If it was really God helping them, shouldn't life be easier? What was this strange new food they were being served? On and on…the whining didn't end until God decided to let them all die out and take a new generation into the land He had promised.

Regret is a debilitating device erected in our hearts and minds to stop us dead in our tracks, to halt our progress and distract us with all the things that will never serve us or empower us to move forward in life. Regret is the land that many live in, unable to get over the walls of the past to occupy the promise, the better, the greater, and the next that is anxiously awaiting them. Like Lot's wife, we have those *if only* moments.

Fact: The problem with *if only* is that it is a suggestion of an option that never really existed. If you were really serious about getting on with life and moving to another level of living and loving, you would not think, *If only…* Such thinking makes you shirk your present responsibilities to live the life you were created for and called to live.

Change is scary and difficult even when we want it, but it's worse when change has been thrust upon us by an adverse or unexpected circumstance. This can leave us in a tailspin that is not easy to rectify. We rehearse the past over and over in our heads, looking for the loopholes that we hope can lead us back to more familiar ground. But the sands have shifted and there is no longer the foothold you need to go back to where you were. And if you did, what would you really find there?

Again, it is our attitude toward disruption that equips us to embrace change and newness in a healthy way that will feed us and strengthen us to thrive in our new setting or situation. God was the first change management specialist. He knew that moving forward cannot be a reality for those who choose to dwell in the past, so He waited for an entirely new generation to come into being before taking the Israelites into the promised land. (See Numbers 32:13.)

When COVID-19 struck the world, it was interesting to see how the church reacted. Some found joy in pivoting to online services and finding creative ways to reach their parishioners and the world at large that was seeking answers about the pandemic. Those who chose to rail against the lockdown and demonize it found themselves floundering and losing members. They withered and died on the vine because they just couldn't wrap their minds around doing church any other way. Yet the same old model of the church was not working in the present climate. It was a different season.

I had interesting conversations with several pastor friends. Some were gleeful about not being in the building. They missed their parishioners but found they were reaching more people online than they had when services were in person. Giving was up, and overhead was down. They were thriving in what seemed to be an unending desert to others. Some concluded that while God did not cause the pandemic, He certainly was using it to His advantage to spread the gospel in a different and unique way. Those who embraced the changes were flourishing and realizing that even after they went back to the church building, their ministries had shifted them to an entirely different way of doing things. It would never be back to the old model of church as usual.

WORKING TO THE GOOD

What seemed like a bad thing had worked to the good to reinvent the way ministry was done, broadening the church's reach and giving them greater effectiveness and fruitfulness. Those who would never step into a church building watched services online. Those who were sitting in dead churches or listening to bad teachers were able to discover amazing and transformational instructors online. Those who weren't grounded in sound theology were struggling. Many believers had to grow up and learn how to find God for themselves. Hero worship was dismantled to a great degree, and the church at large was challenged to grow into maturity. Emotionalism wasn't working, nor was being overly spiritual, because everyone was looking for real answers.

I passionately believe there was a pruning going on within the church—a lifting and separating, a pulling down and a raising up. New voices emerged that were on fire with amazing revelations. They turned the emphasis back to God and His kingdom rather than the building of personal empires. The tide was shifting. The master gardener was doing His best work, cutting back some vines to make room for sweeter, richer crops and removing what was unfruitful. It was time for a new crop. Those who were spiritually sensitive recognized the season and made the proper adjustments, embracing the opportunity to be productive in greater ways.

It's all in how you choose to look at your circumstances and discern what the lesson or new direction is for you. Depending on your perspective, there is always something to be gained. During times like these when newness and change are thrust upon us, instead of panicking, stop and peruse the terrain. Chart your direction. Assess what needs to go and what you need to keep. Pressing the replay button will not serve you at this moment. Imagine a newborn trying to crawl back into the womb of its mother, refusing to be born. Life is waiting. There is only constriction and darkness in the other direction. You are trying to return to a place where you no longer fit. Forget about it. You are no longer who you were. It is time to move forward. New seasons demand new clothing, a new attitude, a new you!

What do you do when God shakes up your normal, when the old mode of doing things no longer works? What do you do when you have to turn right or get left in the dust?

THE POWER OF THE PIVOT

Shift happens in life, and you must master your ability to pivot. Change is inevitable, but how you respond to it is totally in your hands. You must trust and know that how you respond will have everything to do with your outcome. You get to choose if you will be a victim or a victor, a survivor or an overcomer.

Interruptions, intrusions, confusion, and upheaval are never reasons to look back and lose your forward momentum because you are crying over spilled milk. Don't get hung up on what you perceive as negative. Find the gold—the new opportunity, the chance at a new beginning, and the opportunity to experience renewal. All you have to do is shift. Become the master of reinvention! Change management at its best takes the lessons learned forward by utilizing new methodology. No more doing things the same old way. Those who insist on doing that get left behind, fired, or retired! You've got to know when to leave the past behind.

One day, some people brought their friend to Jesus. He was blind and wanted to see. (See Mark 8:22–26.) Jesus took him by the hand, led him outside of the village, and healed his sight. Jesus then asked the man what he saw. The man said he saw men like trees walking around. Jesus touched him again and then he saw things clearly. Seeing men as trees was a distorted view of who others were in comparison to himself. They were bigger than life, diminishing who he was and what he was capable of doing. After a second touch from Jesus, he was able to see everything from the right perspective. Jesus then told him not to go back into the village he had come from. Why? Because that old place would change his thinking back to the old mindset. It would limit his view and affect his ability to see things as he should. New sight brings about a new life. Vision is just the beginning.

Pressing the replay button does not serve us. Moving forward does. We've been told that when the groundhog crawls out of his hole, sees his shadow, and goes back into hibernation, we can look forward to an extended winter. But we are not at the mercy of nature, and we are not victims of circumstance. We are masters of our tomorrow. How we see things, what we choose to cling to, what we decide to discard, and the direction we choose to look has everything to do with reaching our next.

WHEN SHIFT HAPPENS

Responding versus reacting is a healthier space to live in. Choosing not to react out of fear, hurt, or anger will help us get clarity on the way forward. It is not necessary to rush to any conclusion when change is thrust upon you. Stop, breathe, think, seek counsel, pray, wait until the coast is clear, make a decision, and then strategically and purposefully move forward.

MINDSHIFT

- What makes you uncomfortable about moving forward?
- What do you think you will miss? Does it serve you where you are going?
- What do you need to let go of or forget in order to embrace your next?
- What do you anticipate as you move forward?
- How will you feel when it becomes a reality?

HINDSIGHT

What it took to get us where we *were* will not be what it takes to get us where we are going. If we don't grow, we stagnate and die. Growth is the great adventure we fear because we can't always see the other side of it. The fear of becoming is very real. Therefore, the familiar, whether good or bad, seems better than nothing—but it isn't.

Ask yourself this question: If nothing in your life ever changed, how would you feel?

THE NEXT PRAYER

But forget all that—it is nothing compared to what I am going to do. For I am about to do something new. See, I have already begun! Do you not see it?   (Isaiah 43:18–19)

Dear heavenly Father, help! I am stuck. Stuck in the past. I can't seem to help "nursing and rehearsing" things I can do nothing about. I live in a state of constant regret. I replay things gone by again and again, and it only deepens my dissatisfaction. I can't seem to find a way to stop playing the old tape. My mistakes and losses keep playing over and over in my head. I know that I should move forward but I keep looking back, which paralyzes me. I ask that You heal my memories. Help me to forgive myself as I receive Your forgiveness. Thank You for the chance You have given me to begin again and embrace a new beginning. Give me the courage to leave the familiar behind and go where You lead me to higher heights and undiscovered territory. Help me to put regrets in their rightful place behind me as I turn to look at and follow You, in the name of Christ Jesus. Amen.

What do you need to forget? How has it stopped serving you?

_____

_____

_____

_____

What new thing is God trying to introduce you to?

_____

_____

_____

_____

Write your faith confession here:

_____

_____

_____

_____

NINE

KEEP IT MOVING

It's been said there are bigger devils at higher levels. But I will counter that the closer you get to your goal, the more tempting it can be to abort all efforts. This is the place where self-doubt sets in, as do weariness, frustration, even abdication, and apathy—especially if you don't have the right support system in place to keep pumping you up and cheering you on.

Imagine Noah building the ark year after year. There was no sign of impending rain, only a promise. Not even a vision! Just a promise. Yet something deep in Noah's gut drove him forward. One line of study says that Noah prepared by planting trees one hundred and twenty years before he began to build the ark, so that the wood would be available when the time came.

What does this say about us if we cave in at the first sign of delay or setback?

What makes someone keep going when there is no sign of relief in sight?

You guessed it—your cause, your passion, your desire, and, most importantly, your why! Relevance, my music ministry, wrote a song entitled "For Love's Sake" as we pondered why someone would be willing to strip themselves of royalty and practically live a pauper's life. What would make Jesus bear the sin and shame of those He created, die on a rugged cross, and suffer rejection? Only for love's sake would someone go through all of that to redeem the world. Jesus knew His *why*. He didn't come to live; He came to die to redeem all mankind. He made the move from heaven to earth and then to hell to accomplish His mission. Why? Purely out of love—not just for you and me, but for His Father, whose heart's desire was to reconcile us back to Himself so that He could have fellowship with us. Love was His why, and it drove Him forward to complete His task despite having to love the unlovely, the unlovable, and those who could not comprehend or appreciate what He was all about. With His eye on His why, He endured the cross, the rejection, and the betrayal, disregarding the shame of it all. (See Hebrews 12:2.) He reaped the rewards of His efforts—the joy of redeeming humanity. Love is a compelling why.

A popular song starts with this verse:

When a man loves a woman

Can't keep his mind on nothin' else

He'd trade the world

For the good thing he's found[4]

We've heard it and seen it. Love is the driver of sacrifice. Passion and desire fuel us even when we face obstacles.

It is critical to know your *why*! Why are you doing what you're doing? Sometimes there is no explanation because you are being driven from within. Life can also be the catalyst for why you do what you do. The needs of others can be another motivation.

Due to some bad choices of employees at one point in my career, I lost everything: my office, my home, and tons of speaking opportunities, greatly affecting my finances. To top it all off, my father died. I didn't have

---

4. Michael Bolton, "When a Man Loves a Woman," on *Time, Love & Tenderness* (Columbia Records, 1991).

the money to attend his funeral in Ghana, West Africa. I wondered, *Could anything else happen?* It was an overwhelming time as I tried my best to pivot and deal realistically with my circumstances. As concerned friends gathered to see how they could help, I asked one of them, "Aren't you worried about me?" To which she answered, "No, I'm not. You always seem to recover ten paces ahead of where you fell. I'm just waiting to see the comeback. In the meantime, I'm here to help."

With the help of friends, I made it to my father's funeral, only to discover he had left his entire life for me to carry on. I found myself running back and forth from America to Ghana, trying to keep my own life afloat and settle my father's estate at the same time. It was overwhelming and taking its toll on me mentally and physically. Something had to shift. I just wasn't clear on what that was yet.

That being said, I took a deep breath and focused on what I needed to do next. I remember the moment well. I was speaking at a women's conference, and Matthew West was singing the song "The Motions." This verse slammed me between the eyes:

I don't wanna spend my whole life asking

What if I had given everything

Instead of going through the motions?[5]

I felt urged to move to Ghana. I had no idea what I would do there, but I felt so compelled that I knew it was a God call. I could not remain stuck where I was in this middle zone. I had to move forward. The confirmation came from my accountant. She planted her feet in front of my desk and told me that what was happening in my ministry was not sustainable. She suggested I move to Ghana, not do anything for a year, and find out what God wanted to do with my life.

That was it for me. When I announced that I was moving to Ghana, everyone thought I was joking. Yet three weeks later, all my earthly belongings were in a container floating on the Atlantic Ocean while I was flying toward a new adventure with my three dogs. Mind you, I still didn't know what I was heading toward but I felt compelled to keep moving forward.

---

5. Matthew West, "The Motions, on *Something to Say* (Sparrow Records, 2008).

STEPPING OUT IN FAITH

I felt a little bit like Abram in the Bible. When God called him to journey from where he was, He just told Abram to head up and move out. (See Genesis 12:1–6.) I wonder what the conversation was like between him and his wife Sarai.

"Where are we going?"

"I don't really know. God told me to move."

And move they did. Without a backward glance. We are told that Abram left friends, family, and familiar places to obey the voice of God. It propelled him onward even when he didn't know where he would end up. It is said he went seeking a city *"designed and built by God"* (Hebrews 11:10). That is called the walk of faith! It is not by compulsion. When destiny calls, you answer, driven by the voice within, an instinct that tells you this is the way forward. Abram did it, and I did it too. Packed up my life and moved! Was it scary? Mmm… yes and no.

Life will push you to shift in some instances. I really had no other option. I think God set me up. He knew that if things had kept humming along, with a fully booked calendar and money flowing, I most likely would not have moved. He allowed the figurative brook to dry up. It was move or die. Those were my choices. So I took the leap of faith and lived to tell the story. Boy, am I glad I did! Now that I consider my life and the turn of events in retrospect, I can see that things have occurred beyond my wildest dreams that wouldn't have happened anywhere else. Things turned out far better than I could have planned them. I believe Abram, renamed Abraham by God, would second the motion. Abraham not only became extremely wealthy but he gained the legacy of being *"the father of many nations"* (Genesis 17:5). This can only occur if you dare to make that move and keep moving even when the end is not as clear as you would like it to be.

Fact: Sometimes you face only two options: do something and live, or do nothing and die. What have you got to lose? Your future if you don't make a move!

There is a biblical story about four lepers who sat beside the gate of a besieged city that was in a state of famine because of a standoff against its enemy. (See 2 Kings 7:3–11.) The lepers sat and thought about their options. They could either head toward the enemy camp and beg for food or stay where they were and die. They decided they would rather die with full bellies. Upon reaching the camp, however, they discovered it was deserted! They were able to eat, drink, and carry away gold, silver, and clothing that was left behind. The lepers then decided to share the news with the city that was starving and in fear. Their decision to move didn't just benefit them; it helped many others.

Perhaps you've had a vision of where you want to go, what you want to do, and what rewards await you if you persist. It is important to see the vision, write the vision, and follow through persistently and consistently. Besides knowing your *why*, you need to know your *what*. What were you created to do? Who is supposed to be the beneficiary of your giftings and efforts?

Jesus was clear about His audience—the lost, sick, and dying. He knew He had to die to fulfill His mission. He persistently and consistently pursued His path even when it didn't make sense, even when it felt as if He was losing everything.

Instead, He went down to hell, "*led captivity captive*" (Ephesians 4:8 KJV), and made an open show of embarrassing the devil by snatching the keys of hell and death out of his hands! (See Colossians 2:15; Revelation 1:18.) He became sin for a people who rejected, betrayed, and brutalized Him. (See 2 Corinthians 5:21). Causing a breach between Him and His heavenly Father was not the desired path, and yet He was relentless in His decision to see His mission through to the very end. Thank God He did!

You might ask, "Michelle, how do you know you are doing the right thing? If it looks ridiculous and you have no concrete explanation for what you are doing when questioned, how do you know it's a God move and not just a pipe dream or a foolish obsession?"

The answer to that question is to check your peace meter. The beautiful thing about having "*the peace of God, which transcends all understanding*" (Philippians 4:7 NIV) is that you don't have to understand; you just know in your spirit that you are following where God points. The Israelites who followed the cloud by day and a pillar of fire by night on their way to the promised land complained, speculated, and doubted, but they kept moving forward, knowing they were being led by God even against their worst inclinations.

THE SUBSTANCE OF FAITH

All the Israelites in the wilderness had was a promise, without a lot of explanation.

God said, "You are going to a land flowing with milk and honey. Go check it out, scope it out."

They replied, "But how, God? There are giants in the land, things that are sure to block my way, give me pushback, defeat me, or kill me!"

Ever felt that way? Ever notice that God doesn't reveal the *how* until you say yes to the instruction? With the yes comes a peace that God, not you, is capable of fulfilling the promise as He directs you and you cooperate with His instructions. Sometimes even after you've said yes, the entire strategy is still not revealed, lest you get presumptuous and run ahead of Him.

We walk it out by faith as He sheds just enough light for the step we are on. It's His way of pacing us and building our capacity to handle what He plans to entrust to us. Getting it is one thing. Keeping it is another.

The promise and the Promise Keeper will remain true as long as we remain consistent and obedient participants in the plan. When we are in agreement and alignment with God, His peace and certainty become our inward anchor. We move in what my dear friend Marshawn Evans calls "God-fidence." We move forward understanding the assignment and not allowing anyone or anything to stop us, not even our own fears and uncertainty, because the only way to get where we truly want to go is to keep moving!

WHEN SHIFT HAPPENS

It is important to strike a balance between pausing for reflection on the way forward and leaping into action too quickly. Fear of change or failure keeps many of us hostage, circumventing our new beginning. As much as we may want a change, we must be a willing participant in it. A dream without a plan is just a desire. A dream without action is a hope deferred with no one to blame but the inactive dreamer. Change and progress require prayerful dreamers and discernment. It also requires the willingness to take risks, to do what we've never done before. There is no such thing as normal and successful. The difference between those who don't excel and those who do is boiled down to one simple word: action. Persistent, consistent, deliberate action.

MINDSHIFT

+ What actions do you need to take now?
+ What is causing you to delay?
+ What things are distracting you from your desired outcome?
+ What do you need to put in place to help you move forward?
+ What mindset do you need to shift?

HINDSIGHT

You need to know that everything you've experienced, including mistakes and failures, has led you to this moment. It has empowered you to do what you must do now to take your life to the next level. Don't forget the valuable lessons you've learned along the way. They will serve you now as you move into your harvest season. Get rid of regret. It will only paralyze you. Instead, nurture a spirit of gratitude for everything that occurred previously. It's made you who you are today—wiser, stronger, and ready for the task at hand. God doesn't mention the work or the obstacles you will face because they are not an issue to Him. As you partner with Him, you will receive all the wisdom you need to conquer your new territory. Are you ready? Let's do this!

Ask yourself this question: What would you tell your younger self now about what it takes to succeed professionally, relationally, and financially?

THE NEXT PRAYER

Take the prophets as your mentors. They have prophesied in the name of the Lord and it brought them great sufferings, yet they patiently endured. We honor them as our heroes because they remained faithful even while enduring great sufferings. And you have heard of all that Job went through and we can now see that the Lord ultimately treated him with wonderful kindness, revealing how tenderhearted he really is!

(James 5:10–11 TPT)

Dear heavenly Father, I am guilty of sitting down on the job and quitting. I feel as if I don't have the stamina to keep pushing through this. I have tried everything in my own strength to change my situation and I feel as if I am not making progress. I feel defeated. Lost. Without direction. Weary and overwhelmed. I struggle to hear Your voice and Your direction. Perhaps my questions are drowning out Your answers. Strengthen me and give me hope. Then help me to keep pressing forward. Deep in my spirit, I know there is a blessing waiting for me if I can just keep moving! Help me renew my mind to see the new and endless possibilities instead of past defeats. I know You have good plans for me to give me my desired end. I am looking forward to it! As I choose to trust You completely, I am invigorated to keep moving even though everything within me strains against doing so. Continue to guide me with Your eye, in the name of Christ Jesus. Amen.

What things have delayed your progress?

_____

_____

_____

_____

What do you need to do to get back on track?

_____

_____

_____

_____

Write your faith confession here:

_____

_____

_____

_____

SUMMER

can't think of anyone who doesn't look forward to summer. It represents the fullness of life! It is harvest time! After months of hibernation and cold weather that gives way to spring showers, the constant warmth is welcome. People anticipate summer before it arrives. After spring cleaning comes the exhilaration of enjoying outdoor activities. Runs in the park, festivals, barbeques, and get-togethers. The sun makes us feel alive. We get our second wind!

Hopes are renewed. Energy and vitality are revitalized. The motivation to move and do things that have been lying dormant is reactivated! The vitamin D in the sun affects our physical health, and our mental health is revived. Summer is a significant time of strength, fertility, and abundance. This is the season with the longest days and shortest nights. We get more done when the days are longer. We don't tire as easily as we do in the wintertime, with its long periods of darkness.

Sunlight always fills us with hope while the night hours can sap our strength and our resolve. It's almost ironic since we dream in the dark, then allow the darkness of uncertainty to kill those very same dreams. Ah, but when we throw a little light on the subject, we come alive! As we understand the seasons, we learn to accommodate each one by adjusting our mindset and our posture. Attitude is everything.

Seeing the benefits of each season, no matter how unpleasant they may be to you, positions you to be consistent moving forward and grounded in your growth. It's called embracing the process. Ultimately you know that increase is coming, that all the hard work, the sowing and planting, the plotting and planning, the strategizing, the nurturing, and the fertilizing will finally pay off!

Yes, even the seasons have expiration dates. It is lack of knowledge that tends to wear us down, the darkness of not knowing where, when, who, and how our needs will be fulfilled and our dreams realized.

The irony of it all is that we long for summer in winter. We reminisce about days spent in the sun, at the beach, or at our favorite outdoor restaurant or activity. Sometimes we can't appreciate winter's chills because we are too busy longing for the warmth of summer! Yet when summer finally comes, many of us begin to complain about the same heat we said we missed.

If the weather seems to change rapidly, some are not ready for it. They haven't made the transition mentally or physically to be ready to jump into summer with all the gusto it requires. Some are still stuck in spring cleaning mode and haven't unpacked their summer clothes yet. Some people cannot take extreme heat; they wilt while others thrive. We can dream about the harvest, the breakthrough season of our lives better known as summer, but still not be ready.

While anticipating summer, you need to be mentally, spiritually, and physically conditioned to not only celebrate the harvest but withstand the heat that comes with it. The higher the altitude, the thinner the air. You've got to breathe deeply and keep climbing. With every great acquisition or level of achievement, new challenges await you, things that will test your character, your abilities, and even your faith—in yourself as well as God. Can you take the heat?

The heat of success can be greater than the heat of failure. Hopefully, the lessons you've learned in the other seasons have conditioned and prepared you to embrace summer with such grace that no one sees you sweat. Summer is a season that you can enjoy and master or simply end up enduring and imploding based on your expectations and perceptions of what the season is supposed to look like.

Assess where you are and gain clarity:

+ What does success look like to you?

+ What would make you feel like you had finally arrived?

+ What is the purpose of success?

+ Why do you want to be successful?

+ Once you succeed, then what?

When we focus on how to be a wise steward of our harvest, we find ourselves in a place of abundance that will not only be a blessing to us but a benefit to others. The common adage, "We are blessed to be a blessing" reveals an important principle. Some of the most successful and wealthy people in the world are philanthropists who use their platform and their wealth to affect change where needs are apparent.

The summer of our lives is not just about fun in the sun, breakthroughs, harvests, and enjoying life. It is about something more lasting. It is about feeding others. It's not just about what we get in that season; it is about what we give. Creating legacy. Channeling resources the right way. Summer is the season of favor, provision, and restoration. What we do in this season has everything to do with how long it will last.

Those who sow with tears will reap with songs of joy. Those who go out weeping, carrying seed to sow, will return with songs of joy, carrying sheaves with them. (Psalm 126:5–6 NIV)

TEN

GET YOUR SHIFT TOGETHER

One year, I lived in California for what I will call my personal winter. I couldn't win to save my life...or so it appeared at the time. Looking back, I called it "the best of times and the worst of times," like the famous Charles Dickens novel, *A Tale of Two Cities*.

It was the worst of times because I went in pursuit of love only to discover it was not there for me. He had moved on, and I was perpetually stuck in what could have been. I was an emotional wreck, living under the delusion that if I hung around long enough, he would see the error of his ways and realize that I was the woman for him—a long and painful lesson. But that's another book. It was also the worst of times because the "friends" who had encouraged me to move to California were suddenly unavailable. I was only valuable to them when I was in the position to hire them for commercials at my fabulous advertising job. Now that I was unemployed... well, you know the rest. There I was on my own with no support system in a new environment. The only friend I had went off to Europe, leaving me behind to navigate my way around a new city, a new environment, and a new life.

I was striking out in the job market as well, which led to financial complications. My little nest egg quickly ran out, leaving me in a state I had never experienced before: I was broke! Broke and broken. For someone who had grown used to living a lavish life in the world of advertising—where you are courted and gifted by representatives of film directors and photographers, and fine foods, trinkets, and the hottest tickets to events in town are pretty much cast at your feet—the silence of no admirers was deafening and destabilizing. When I shared stories of my glory days with my new friends, they looked at me as if to say, "Poor thing. She has an overactive imagination." All I had left were memories of better days, a car that flooded every time it rained, a broken heart, and a million questions for God.

LIVING IN HINDSIGHT

Looking back, it all seems so ridiculous to me. I think of all the things I could have been doing and the opportunities I could have explored. I could kick myself. I was so myopic. In my mind, I was the golden art director, writer, and producer at the largest black advertising company in the U.S. For some reason, that made me overqualified at the agencies I had applied to in Los Angeles. Nevertheless, I got stuck on who I was and lost sight of who I could become. It never occurred to me that there were other things I could do. I could have modeled—after all, an agency had sought me—but no, I was an advertising creative. I *hired* models; I didn't wait to be chosen as one. Plus, I didn't want to watch my weight. I could have done voiceovers, but I was intimidated by my environment. I didn't really know where to turn or what all of my options were. I didn't have the courage to approach the production houses. This was L.A., where all the famous people took all the jobs. Why would they want to hire me? I could have offered my services to freelance ad agencies, but no, I had to have a *permanent* nine-to-five job security. I forgot that freelance work was how I landed the first job I had. I considered myself above and beyond that.

So you can guess where all of this left me. Nowhere. My thoughts were scattered and finding no harbor. Oblivious to suggestions that didn't fit into the box I was in, I floundered and failed miserably at moving forward. What could have been an amazing new beginning became a miserable experience. I was all about surviving my present without casting a vision for my future. The truth of the matter was I couldn't because I wasn't aware of what I had to work with!

Once upon a time, there was a widow who lived during a time of drought and famine. Elijah the prophet visited her and asked for some food. (See 1 Kings 17:8–15.) She told him she just had *"a handful of flour...and a little cooking oil in the bottom of the jug"* (verse 12). She planned to prepare one last meal for herself and her son to eat before they died. The prophet told her to prepare a small loaf of bread for him first and then another for herself and her son. If she did this, Elijah assured her, she would not run out of flour and oil until it began to rain again. The widow did as he instructed her, and his word proved to be true. They had an endless supply of flour and oil, enough to feed her, her family, and Elijah until the drought was over and crops grew again.

The challenge was looking past her own personal need to focus on someone else in need, opening the floodgates of provision for her. Can you imagine her joy level when this happened? To think she was at the end of her provision only to discover that as she used what she had to benefit someone other than herself, she was actually going to experience abundance. This had to be a great revelation on the economy of God. In times of lack, if you seek to be of service to someone, what you seek will find you! As this poor widow shifted focus, her conditions shifted. This is a principle that is critical to learn!

THE RIGHT ACCESS

This widow had no idea of the power that was in her hand. So many of us are like that. We don't realize what we are packing and the endless possibilities we possess if we can just look past where we presently stand and what we have at the moment. If we can stop to give thought to what is available to us and what options those things present, we will be able to construct a plan and see our way forward. God is a God of reinvention. As we discover the endless possibilities we house within ourselves, we can step out of our personal boxes and enlarge our store of provision as well as our territory and our sphere of influence. The widow's willingness to serve gave her access to someone others longed to know.

Fact: The danger of not knowing what you carry, the value of your gifts, and how to shift when life changes can rob you of valuable opportunities. Life is never static; circumstances are never fixed. While we desire changes, greener pastures, higher levels, and a greater impact on our world, these come at a cost.

Nothing new can start until the old is discarded. Some have the luxury of easing into a new season and direction. At one point, I had that luxury when I transitioned from advertising to ministry. I had done several voice-overs for huge clients, and the residuals were rolling in. I was given the time and finances needed to gain momentum in my new career as an author and speaker without the pressure of working full-time and trying to nurture my dream part-time. But everyone doesn't have that experience. For many, the change is like a Chicago spring—hot one minute and cold the next, catching you off guard in the wrong attire for the elements.

If you've weathered all of the other seasons, there is a valuable lesson to learn about something that precedes all change, whether positive or negative. That is called process. Yes, there is a tension that exists between where you are, where you are going, and where you ultimately end up. This is why breaks occur. It is the process to get to the next. Even Jesus had to be broken to make the transition from God to man and back again to His former glorified state. God the Father blessed His Son, then He broke Him, and then He gave Jesus Christ for the sake of all mankind.

Anything you regard as precious was processed, crushed, broken, cut, ground, or made to look completely insignificant, even worthless, before it took on the state you have come to value. Olives are pressed for their oil. Roses are crushed for their perfume. Gold is melted down completely to remove all impurities. Diamonds are cut, shaped, and polished to gain their brilliance. This begs the question of why we lean more to the side of what we've done wrong than what we are about to do when we experience the process of becoming.

Have you ever asked yourself, "What did I do wrong?" or wondered if God had forsaken you because He was mad at you? Have you questioned your own abilities when life seemed to go south? I am reminded of an old ad campaign, "Why ask why?" Yes, why ask why this is happening? Will it change your circumstances?

What happens if you change the question? I've often said that God doesn't answer very often when we ask, "Why?"—but ask Him, "What?" and you get a stream of information. The truth of the matter is this: God doesn't waste your setbacks. He uses them to strengthen you, teach you, redirect you, and give you experience that will not leave you wanting again…if you let Him, that is.

This is where we make the aggressive choice to yield to the process, squeeze our pain, and ask the right questions so we can use the answers we receive to move forward with grace. Not as victims, but as people expecting greater and higher levels of life.

You might be thinking, *What are you saying, Michelle? Should I just roll over when life is literally squeezing the life out of me?* I hear you. No, that is not what I'm saying at all! I'm not telling you to roll over. I'm telling you to lean in. Lean into what life is telling you. Lean into what your disappointment is revealing to you. Lean into what your pain is forcing you to look at. Lean into the direction your roadblocks are forcing you to take. Lean in! Lean into what you've never considered before. Examine your options completely and realistically. Allow yourself to lean into the process of being blessed, broken, and given. It's all good. Wait for it. The experience is taking you somewhere. At the end of the day, it's actually taking you where you want to go! It just wasn't the route that you expected.

THE HEART OF GOD

God Himself intends to bless you with what you desire. Why? Because He put those desires inside you. He will always answer Himself and bless what He has purposed for your life. This is the reason that living in sync with Him is crucial. Nothing can be more frustrating than harboring a bunch of desires that God never signed off on. Believe me, that never ends well. God says, *"I know the plans I have for you…plans to prosper you and not to harm you, plans to give you hope and a future"* (Jeremiah 29:11 NIV). But what precedes that level of blessing is brokenness.

When a perfume bottle is broken, the air is filled with its heady fragrance. We would never have this experience if the cap had stayed on, and the bottle had remained intact.

I shared the story of how I got fired from my fabulous advertising job. Sometimes shifts disguised as bad things are used to disrupt you and push you to the next level, a place where you will see what you carry in a different light because you never had to utilize it the way you need to use it now. You saw things one way, and God wants to expand your view of the possibilities as well as your abilities. You may have been coasting for a long time in your comfort zone while God wants to move you forward and upward, full speed ahead. He wants to take your life to another level.

My boss accused me of being too comfortable and lazy to pursue my other dreams. The truth of the matter is, she was right. I have had this repetitive dream over the years about living in a house that I thought was beautiful, spacious, and enough for me. Then one day as I'm looking for something, I discover there are more rooms in a section of my home that I never knew about! I get so excited about finding these additional spaces that I start planning how I can utilize them. Then, just before I wake up, I say, "If only I had known about these rooms before. I could have done so many things with them." I interpret this as God telling me there is more to me than I know. That house is me and there are things in me—giftings, capabilities, and creativity—that I haven't discovered yet. I should never settle for where I am. I should remain curious because there is always more.

My boss knew I was comfortable. I will go further: I had grown stagnant. Meanwhile, I had started writing a book two years before this, but my job kept me distracted. I had never even moved past the first chapter; I was too busy coming up with clever hooks—tag lines and catch phrases—for cars, soda, and french fries. But suddenly, all of that was gone. I had to consider my options. What was within my reach? What internal resources could I utilize? I ended up doing two projects for my former employer that paid more money than my old full-time salary. I also gained an additional skill set as a director, and I won awards for both pieces of work. I did voiceover work and freelanced for other agencies. But still, something was missing.

A SHIFT IN TIME

Then it happened. On the way to a voiceover audition, I was hit by a car, as I mentioned previously. My body was broken. I was broken. Three surgeries and a year and a half in bed don't really help your morale. Being helpless has never been on my list of things I would like to do. On the one hand, I found out who all my friends were; on the other hand, I felt bad having to depend on them. It was a humbling experience. I had a lot of time to think about my life while I was flat on my back. Between learning to walk again and having to submit to my friends' ministrations, I had to consider my options. What was in my hand?

Now that I couldn't do all the things I used to do, the door was being opened for something new. All I had to do was step through it! In my brokenness, a new life was pushing through the shattered parts with the promise of something beautiful, more valuable, more enriching and fulfilling, above and beyond my dreams—dreams I had tucked away in my *someday* file. Little did I know that someday had arrived.

Brokenness, famine, and drought are beautiful things because they remove all of the other silly distractions and make you focus on what is truly needful. What is really important. What matters in the long term. It also fine-tunes your vision to what you have at hand that you may have overlooked before or whose value you may have failed to discern.

What I had in my hand was the ability to write. After working at an ad agency for years, I learned how to share my words and my heart effectively. My body may have been limited and housebound, but my mind was not! What was within me was greater than my external abilities or disabilities. This taught me a valuable lesson.

Fact: What we consider dead ends are most certainly detours to a better life and a better you. There is no such thing as an end, only a next!

In light of where you are right now, I challenge you to think of all the things you take for granted that others appreciate or take note of about you. I want you to prayerfully consider that thing or things that can work for you in this season of your life. I dare to say that if you are at a place where you are wondering what could possibly be *next*, summer is closer than you think. Spring may have looked promising but it's still filled with delays because of all the things involved in getting you ready for the harvest coming your way. It will always take divine disruption for change to be ushered in. It will always take a degree of brokenness to reveal what is really inside of you, to not only expose the precious, but also to strengthen you to be able to stand the heat.

You see, I have a small confession. I was not ready for the heat of success when it overtook me. In all honesty, I was literally swept off my feet when my first book, *What to Do Until Love Finds You*,[6] was released. Twelve thousand copies were gone in three weeks! Another publishing contract, a flurry of television and radio interviews, and invitations to speak here, there, and everywhere followed—it was all pretty heady stuff. My brokenness kept me grounded...it couldn't possibly be me; it had to be God. I never saw it coming, and yet, here was summer, filled with a harvest of offers. I scrambled to keep up.

WHEN THE HEAT IS ON

All of this to ask: Are you ready for summer? Consider the seeds you've planted and the ones you've held onto out of fear that you lacked the knowledge to grow them. There is more inside of everyone, more that has yet to be discovered. Trial, upheaval, and brokenness are the vehicles of growth, change, and the realization of all that has been deposited within you. The shifts and disruptions separate fact from fiction, waste from the useful, and distraction from divine design and order.

Sometimes we have to be shocked into taking a hard look at what we are working with in order to craft a plan to be fruitful.

Yes! A plan is necessary. Those who don't make plans plan to fail. There is no way I would ever embrace the theory of evolution. Things deteriorate when they are left to their own devices. The mind is the only thing that evolves. When we become so distracted by what we desire to occur that we fail to plan what to do, we may be left in a worse state than before. I believe this is the reason why seasons and processes exist. God wants us to be ready to handle all that comes our way with grace and consistent peace. He wants us to be able to maintain and sustain what we attain.

---

6. Michelle McKinney Hammond, *What to Do Until Love Finds You: The Bestselling Guide to Preparing Yourself for Your Perfect Mate* (Eugene, OR: Harvest House Publishers, 1997).

Fact: There is a rhythm to mastering summer so that you get the best out of yourself and the season. Pacing yourself is important.

Most artists and successful people toil for a long time to achieve their dreams. Years pass when it seems like nothing is occurring, then all of a sudden, fortune favors them. They become an *overnight success*. No one is privy to all the work that went on underground before the fruit of their labor goes on display to the world. They go viral!

In the heat of the moment, even you can forget what it took to get there as you get caught up in the tide of success and all it brings. Everyone wants all of what you have to offer, along with a piece of you. Literally, you can be consumed by all of this, or you can ride the wave and gracefully land with sustainable success in hand.

When I visited my mother's native country of Barbados, I loved to go to the beach and sit out in the sun for hours on end. I lived for the sand, the sea, and the beautiful tan I would get as proof of my vacation. As I lay on my towel listening to music, shortly before noon, the little old ladies would saunter by, shielded from the sun's rays by wide-brimmed straw hats. In their musical voices, they would warn me, "Darling, you better come out de sun before you get sunstroke!" They knew the danger of too much heat. They understood that the healing virtues of the sun could also turn lethal due to overexposure. Being uncovered and vulnerable when the sun reaches its zenith is not good. It leads to dehydration, severe headaches, and even death if it's a hot, bright, sunny day.

What am I saying? Forget about, "Can you stand the rain?" My question is, "Can you stand the heat?" Do you know when to put yourself out there and when to take cover? Do you know how to seek the balance between success and sanity? God wants you to have success, but success should never have you. It should never become the definition or the driver of who you are. All the things you've dreamed of accomplishing are not who you *are*. They are what you *do*, which can shift over time.

THE CHANGING FACES OF FAITH

This is where a lot of celebrities and successful people lose it, even pastors and workers in ministry. The heat, the roar of the crowd, and the excitement of promotion can wipe us out if we are not grounded. If we tried to skip one of the previous seasons or failed to see the point of what we went through, our fruit will not be sustained. We will begin to produce corrupted fruit, tainted by flesh and shipwrecked lives.

I have concluded that in this hour, the church has split into two camps or models. There are those with deep roots who are solid, grounded, on point, and uncompromising with the Word of God. The General Motors model, if you will. They can go the distance, tried and true, fueled by the Holy Spirit they still rely on for oil. Then there is the sleek, shiny model—attractive, streamlined, modern, and fast. It draws a lot of attention and doesn't depend on fuel; it has to plug in to go the distance. They are electric! These are the Teslas, the wave of the future. Their ministries are all flash and surface. Some have substance, but a large portion do not. It's all face value and the wow factor. They draw a lot of attention and don't depend on fuel; they forget they need to plug in to go the distance. They are gifted but lack integrity. They have charisma but lack character. When their moral shortcomings are exposed, they play on the sympathy of the masses, making excuses that dismiss the power of Jesus to transform. Just like Samson, summer has overwhelmed them and caused them to forget their purpose and not respect their calling. They call it being relevant. I wonder what God calls it. If one is not mindful, it is easy to go from being relevant to reprobate without being aware of it until the grace lifts. Like Samson, who got up from a tryst with Delilah. He thought, *"I'll go out as before and shake myself free"* (Judges 16:20 NIV). He didn't realize that the Spirit of the Lord had left him! Scary...

Summer will test your stamina. It will test your character and your morals. It will quickly reveal if you are fit for the battle, in it to win, and conditioned for longevity. Summer can be a major blessing, but it can also be a critical test.

Summer is not the time to relax. It is the time to streamline your mind to focus on your destiny and everything it takes to fulfill it in excellence.

WHEN SHIFT HAPPENS

Hold up! Don't get too excited. Stay in gratitude, but also stay focused. If you're distracted by your successes, you set yourself up to miss important cues. Your discernment concerning the things that can pull you off course is diminished, and costly mistakes that can rob you of your harvest begin to happen. Be cognizant of who you are, what you carry, and the reason you are on the earth. Stay committed to the mission. Get over yourself, remain grateful, and walk in humility. Don't think more highly of yourself than you should, for that is the root of deception. Remember, all glory goes to God. You are a conduit of His purpose, will, and plan.

MINDSHIFT

+ What do you dream about?
+ What will your response be when these things occur?
+ What is your plan for sustaining and growing this achievement?
+ What things could sidetrack you?
+ What mindset do you need to have to stay on course?

HINDSIGHT

Things don't always spring up where you plant them. The root travels from the seed and leads to unexpected adventures and self-revealing occurrences. The things we dream about were never meant to define us or assess our value or what we bring to the table of life. Our achievements were designed to serve mankind and expand the kingdom of God. Every season will point to this cause. We must not forget who we serve and why we do what we do when promotion comes.

Ask yourself this question: What if your summer doesn't look like what you expected? How will you handle it moving forward?

THE NEXT PRAYER

This doesn't mean, of course, that we have only a hope of future joys—we can be full of joy here and now, even in our trials and troubles. Taken in the right spirit, these very things will give us patient endurance. This, in turn, will develop a mature character, which produces a steady hope that will never disappoint us. (See Romans 5:3–5.)

Dear heavenly Father, I sometimes wonder where all of this is going and why it is necessary. Then You tell me it is for my good, my growth, the deepening of my character. I don't always see it that way because it doesn't feel good, and yet I see the outcome on the other side of my trial. I learn with every new development that You remain faithful to get the best out of me. You have given me everything I need to overcome the things that challenge me. Help me to overcome my tendency to abdicate and wait for You to rescue me. Help me to use what You have given me to master my circumstances. May my hope be kept intact so that I patiently await a positive end. Help me to maintain the right spirit in the name of Christ Jesus. Amen.

What things rock your faith and reduce your hope?

_____

_____

_____

_____

What parts of your character need to mature? Why?

_____

_____

_____

_____

Write your faith confession here:

_____

_____

_____

_____

ELEVEN

MASTER THE CYCLE

I have stood capriciously on the brink of overwhelming success only to find myself blown backward by a sudden gust of wind—most commonly known as a setback—several times. I have made a lot of money and lost a lot of money. Been close to the marriage altar only to see the relationship dissolve. Is anybody feeling me on this? Can I get a witness? Some may call it spiritual warfare. I call it seasons. There are storms in every season. Spring has its tornadoes. Summer has its hurricanes. Fall has its thunderstorms from the clash between cold, dry air and warm, humid air that changing seasons bring. Winter has its blizzards. How we weather the storm and the season has everything to do with our outcome, especially when it keeps reoccurring.

You've been there. You've made it safely through your season and given a sigh of relief. Yes, you made it and lived to tell about it. So, what is this? How have you found yourself seemingly back in the same place? Nature follows the natural law of the spirit. Just as the seasons repeat year after year, the seasons come and go in our lives. How many times? As many times as is necessary for us to bear the fruit we were created to give to the world.

Let me help you here. Seasons reoccur, but how you weather them needs to change. The first time you experience spring, you may not know that it rains often, so you get drenched. The next time spring comes, you are aware that it rains, and you are ready for it. You get a raincoat or an umbrella. It can make the difference between you dancing in the rain or running from it.

Fact: Each repetitive season should give you tools that deepen your wisdom, make you more resilient, and bring you to full maturity. It's been said that you should never be afraid to start over again because you are not starting from scratch; you are starting from experience.

THE PURPOSE OF IT ALL

Every season has a purpose. It does not exist apart from the methodology of God. The sooner we can discern the purpose of the season rather than taking it as a personal attack, the faster we will be able to take advantage of the season and emerge better for the experience.

A friend told me of an encounter he had with a woman who was dressed in a heavy coat on a broiling hot day. When he stopped to ask her if she was okay, she became defensive. She complained about people always asking her if she was okay—as if *they* were wrong and she was in the right. It was obvious that she was oblivious to the fact that she was not dressed for the season, giving rise to concern for her.

Not owning where we are can put us in a place of endangerment or simply halt our progress. It stops us from receiving the blessings that we yearn for. Even worse, we then fail to recognize opportunities, available help, and divine connections.

Perceiving, understanding, and mastering your season enables you to reach your desired outcome through a consistent, steady progression rather than emotional high highs and low lows. It will free you from anxiety, frustration, and yes, even depression. Instead of thinking, *Here we go again*, you'll be telling yourself, "Wow, here is another opportunity to master what I missed last time."

There is always a lesson in the season. When we embrace those lessons, the season begins to work for us. We get to take advantage of the season rather than fear it.

I shared with you how I got fired from my advertising job. But it wasn't the first time. It was the second time. Yes! The same place fired me twice. The first time I was *let go* from my job—a gentler way of saying *fired*—I lacked understanding. I wasn't mature. I was a problem. I didn't take corrections well. My ego got in the way of my understanding that I was an employee. I worked for them; they didn't work for me. Imagine my shock when in the midst of all my self-perceived brilliance, I was fired.

I didn't handle this brilliantly at all. I went into survival mode without considering the way forward. I flailed. I failed until I finally fell into a heap, crying out to God for help and direction. A year later, after being totally broken, I was given the opportunity to return to work with my former employer. I went back with a different posture, humbled and understanding that I was there to serve, not be served. My posture toward my work changed. I became more effective at making my boss and clients happy. I learned how to give others what they wanted while maintaining my creative integrity. I no longer saw requests to change my ideas as an insult but as a challenge to make my idea even better than it was before. I stopped being resistant and became more flexible. I went from being a problem child to a favored employee. In hindsight, I thank God for my wilderness season. Lack and a year-long glimpse of being jobless gave me a new appreciation for the job I had, no matter its challenges. It was a painful lesson learned.

GAINING NEW PERSPECTIVE

The second time I was let go, I had a different approach and response. I knew what my capabilities were. I was at peace with leaving, believing it was a good thing designed to let me take advantage of my freedom to pursue my dreams. What I saw as punishment the first go-round, I now saw as a kiss from God and a new season filled with endless possibilities.

It's been said attitude is everything. Mindset comes from attitude. Is the glass half empty or half full? You tell me. When it comes to your life, is it setback after setback? Or is it opportunity after opportunity to dig deeper into yourself to uncover hidden gifts and the vast capacity you have to do more than you've been doing? Could it be that what you see as rejection is redirection?

What's the difference between two people who have faced the same challenge and yet one overcomes it while the other does not? The answer is simple: mindset. What we establish as belief systems will fuel our actions.

We live in a culture that tells you to follow your feelings. Don't do that—at least not until you have analyzed those feelings. A feeling comes from a thought that seeks to establish itself as a belief. Once that belief takes root, it generates an action or a series of actions that will then determine your fate. The problem is that some thoughts are based on assumptions or knee-jerk reactions or triggers from past experiences that may prevent you from accurately reading a given situation. My mother used to say the word *assume* makes an A** out of YOU and ME. (Check the spelling.) Therefore, it is critical not to make decisions when you are hurt, angry, afraid, or sad. Let the smoke clear. Examine the thought behind the feeling. Get your imagination out of the way if it's keeping you from seeing the truth. Get rid of self-defeating thoughts and assumptions. Is that thought true? Does it have any merit? On what grounds? Where is the evidence? Only after answering all of these questions are you free to make clear, educated choices moving forward.

After you've determined the proper response versus a reaction to what you are facing, you must make sure your motivation is clear as well. Why are you doing what you are doing? Who is served by what you choose to do? What is the outcome that you want? Are you self- involved or solution-oriented? Your motivation should be in alignment with your season in order to make sense. There is a time for everything and a purpose for every season. The right move at the wrong time can seem like the wrong move at any time and cost you dearly.

Even when it comes to our words, there is a time to say what you have to say based on the effect you want those words to have. Voiced at the wrong time, they will only get you misunderstood or ignored. Just because you feel it now doesn't mean you should say it now. The listener might not be prepared to receive what you have to say, and your words could have unintended consequences.

Sometimes the atmosphere and conditions around you need to be primed and prepared to receive what you want to offer. A word spoken in the right manner at the right time and in the right setting can be priceless, gleaning a bigger harvest than what you sought. In the same way, even the right word spoken at the wrong time in the wrong place can destroy a relationship, a business deal, or a critical alignment. Are you getting the picture? Timing is everything. It can have a lasting impact, positive or negative.

MASTERING YOUR MINDSET

Your mindset has everything to do with the moves you make. Based on what you believe, you will feel compelled to do something, but there is a difference between a reaction and a response. A reaction generates a thoughtless action based on what is occurring in your life, like the automatic kick you give when a doctor taps the bottom of your knee with a reflex hammer. You lash out against the events or words that were spoken without measuring what has taken place to see if it is even worthy of a response. As William Shakespeare wrote in *Hamlet*, "Give every man thy ear, but few thy voice." Not everything needs to be said. Sometimes your silence says more than words and leaves no room for misinterpretation. When you do speak, let it be a word seasoned with grace and understanding.

A celebrity was recently asked about her gracious response to another celebrity who spoke disparagingly about her. She said she failed to react initially because she really didn't care. However, after some time, she felt the nudge of God to respond on social media. Her tender and loving response became a teachable moment to the world on how to handle offense and made her go viral in a good way. The floodgates opened for her. After years of working at her craft and investing in her dreams, it seemed like her influence blew up overnight. But that wasn't the case. Instead, she had persevered through seasons of lack, rejections, and delays. It was now her season. One amazingly beautiful response amid an ugly situation was the catalyst for thousands to fall in love with her, her brand, and all she had to offer, paving the way for remarkable success and the fulfillment of her dreams.

Our reaction or response can make or break us. Maturity and practice get us to the place where we can be quick to listen, slow to speak, and reluctant to become angry. Consider what sets you off. What makes you spiral? What makes you explode? There will always be an occasion to react inappropriately. Life happens. How you deal with it is up to you. Emotional intelligence and life mastery are things we all can possess. It's our choice.

BEING A CHANGE AGENT

In most situations, it's not what you do but how you do it. The gracious celebrity's response became a catalyst for change. Even in the Word of God, we see many stories where the right response saved lives while the wrong response cost others dearly, where the approach to those who could be of assistance laid the foundation for whether they would be a friend or foe.

One of the most classic examples of this is Queen Esther going before the Babylonian king Xerxes to plead for the lives of her people. (See Esther 7:1–6.) It was an urgent matter, yet with an amazing amount of divine strategy, she served two banquets to the king and her enemy before bringing up the issue, even though Xerxes had asked her three times what he could do for her. By the time she did ask, her words were measured and struck his heart with an accuracy that accomplished her goal. Not only were her people saved but her own position was elevated, and she was well-compensated.

In a society where everyone is quick to share their feelings and voices become more strident about living in "their truth," there is a rising intolerance for anything that opposes a person's position. The yin and yang of life are no longer celebrated. The sad truth is that if we were all alike, not everyone would be necessary. God is a God of diversity. In some way, even the things we don't see as positive bring a balance to the universe. It's called checks and balances. It challenges who we are, the level of our integrity, and the depth of our character. This too is a season that must be discerned, when we decide on the fruit that we want to produce. The signs of the times are upon us.

How you say what you say and how you do what you do makes all the difference in the world. There is the danger of standing on principle and finding yourself standing alone if the foundation of your delivery is wrong. When people like you, they won't help you, and when people don't help you, it hurts you. Mastering being gracious and allowing people to keep their dignity even when you don't agree goes a long way.

When people are empowered to do right by you and for you, the results are notably greater. Seasoned words and actions in season open the door for positive and lasting outcomes that not only bless you but usually have a lasting impact on others. Don't allow yourself to be *triggered* into missing the shift in your season. Remain consistent and sensitive to your inner leading. Recognize that before a major positive shift occurs in your life, a moment of temptation can pull you out of the spirit and off your mark. It will assault you, blindside you, and rock you. Remain steady. Remain grounded. Anticipate that this is your season for renewal and restoration. Don't allow anyone or anything to rob you of your new beginning. Give yourself nothing to regret and everything to celebrate. Don't be distracted by nonessentials. Decide what really matters and stay focused on that. Remember that you made it when you thought that you wouldn't, but also remember not to repeat your missteps.

One of the greatest opportunities we have in every season is to learn from the former one. Yes, seasons reoccur, and we all face repeat cycles. However, not all of these repeats are healthy ones. Being able to glean lessons from former seasons so that our next season is progressively greater is critical to the process of maturity and growing into greatness.

Fact: Let's be clear. Some seasons repeat themselves because we haven't learned the lesson. That is not healthy. Some things are subconsciously lulling us into unproductive habits that keep inviting the same outcomes in our lives.

BREAKING THE CYCLE

If you keep doing the same things over and over, you cannot expect different results. If you are ready to break the cycle and move on to a new season, it's time to own your stuff and take a good hard look at what is causing you to arrive at the same destination every time—where everything looks the same and only the names and faces change. This is how you master the shifts in your life. The shift is an invitation for renewal.

This can happen in relationships, professions, finances, and even our daily life. How many of us have repeatedly dated people with similar personalities? Their names, sizes, shapes, and colors may be different, but the same behavior occurs, bringing yet another painful end. How many of us have switched jobs only to encounter yet another boss just like the last one who we could not stand—only this one is even worse! Or how about those of us who have lost the same twenty pounds repeatedly only to find ten additional pounds? These are seasons we create within seasons based on what else is going on with us at the time.

Check yourself in those vulnerable moments when you are most open to making choices that won't serve you long-term. You know what I'm talking about. That person you already know isn't right for you but fills the gap for now. Something isn't always better than nothing. Or how about comfort food when you are feeling low, unhappy, or dissatisfied? Or going on a shopping spree despite your debt?

These repeat cycles of less-than-stellar behavior actually create unnecessary seasons in our lives. Our refusal to examine our own attitudes and the manner in which we do what we do causes us to repeat the same lesson until we pass the test and graduate to the next level.

Repeated cycles and seasons reveal what we have either ignored or failed to surrender. They expose areas of brokenness and point to where we need to get either wisdom, maturity, or healing. We can't shrink back from that. Truth is the agent that gives us the capacity to attain the freedom and wholeness we long for. In light of this fact, every season is good even when it feels bad because of what it ultimately produces if we let it do its work. Problems help us develop endurance and strengthen our character; this will always produce hope and the expectation of a positive outcome. This is what experience and maturity produce. It gives us the capacity to respond in a healthy manner instead of reacting. It helps us pivot when the next shift occurs, no longer ruled by emotion. Our ability to make sound and wise choices emerges to meet every season with grace.

WHEN SHIFT HAPPENS

Yes, it's easy to have an allergic reaction to occurrences in life that we don't like or anticipate. We literally break out! Our emotions are not the only things affected. We can react physically with illness, anxiety, sweat, and a host of other reactions that will never be the solution to the things we face.

This is where you stop, count to ten if you must, get quiet, pray, still your soul, and do a deep reflection. Let truth settle in your inner parts. Breathe. There is always a solution. There is always a next.

MINDSHIFT

- What does this season look like for you?
- What valuable lessons are you learning from what is happening?
- How will you use what you've learned as you move forward?
- What outcome do you want? What will you do to make that happen?
- What do you need to let go of in order for this to happen?

HINDSIGHT

Seasons should never be seen as a state of emergency. They should be viewed as normal occurrences that pop up at strategic times in our lives to make us, not break us. How the season ends will have everything to do with how we greet it and the spirit with which we embrace it.

Treat the season you are in as a friend and learn all you can while anticipating your next. Ask yourself this question: How have I reacted in the past that didn't serve me? In light of what I know now, how can I respond differently this time?

THE NEXT PRAYER

Restore our fortunes, LORD, as streams renew the desert. Those who plant in tears will harvest with shouts of joy. They weep as they go to

plant their seed, but they sing as they return with the harvest.
(Psalm 126:4–6)

Dear heavenly Father, I stand in hope that as I weather this season of my life, I will bear fruit. Though I have wept bitter tears and questioned why certain things had to happen, I cling to my faith in You, believing that things will work out for my good, that I will get a testimony out of this that will reveal Your goodness. Do not forsake me. Remember me in this season as I try my best to stay faithful to the things before me. Don't let my tears be in vain. Honor the seeds that I have planted in my life, my business, and my relationships. I realize there are ebbs and flows in everything in life. Help me to stand firm when shaken, consistent even as I vacillate between believing in a great outcome and wondering if I deserve it, or if You will be there for me. I know what Your Word promises. Help me to believe and enlarge my capacity to receive all that You have for me in the name of Christ Jesus. Amen.

How do you feel about where you are right now?

_____

_____

_____

_____

What do you hope to harvest in this season of your life?

_____

_____

_____

_____

Write you faith confession here:

_____

_____

_____

_____

TWELVE

WHAT'S NEXT?

Welcome to this thing called life. Life happens. Shift happens. That is the reality we all must face. Perhaps we sometimes feel blindsided. The unexpected can really rock us. There is no Lamaze class for life. But when you stop and think about it, life is sort of like pregnancy. Most of us are unaware of what we are carrying, the endless possibilities and potential that await us on the other side of carrying this weighty thing within us, then enduring labor and finally giving birth to something that makes us forget the former pain. It is truly a process, especially when we are thrown by the things we do not anticipate. I said, "One day, I will write a book about all the things my mother didn't tell me." Can I get a witness?

As children, we long for the day we will grow up, be independent, and do things our own way. No one told us what that would cost us. No one told us about the various seasons of life and how they would impact us in various ways. No one told us about the realities of pain, disappointment, rejection, heartbreak, illness, seeming failure, or aging!

No one told you about the seasons of *almost* where you would get within an inch of your dreams and see them dissipate before you, causing you to wonder if they could ever be a reality. Joseph—the one with the coat of many colors (see Genesis 37:3 KJV)—went through that. He had a dream and then watched everything that was the opposite of that dream occur for years before it finally came true. The ironic part of it all was that his dream was not what he expected. It was bigger than he imagined. It actually had nothing to do with his personal agenda and everything to do with the welfare of countless others. (See Genesis 45:7.) Little did he know what he was being groomed for in the midst of all the setbacks he experienced. Anticipate the same in your life as you wonder if your vision is a mere pipe dream.

No one told you about waiting it out. No one told you what it would take to get to your next—the persistence, the patience, the hope, the faith, the determination, the endurance, the reality checks, and the courage. If they had told you, I wonder if you would have listened. I wonder if you would have still wanted what you wanted!

THE VALUE OF EXPERIENCE

There is something inside of us that makes us feel we are exempt from the reliable experiences of others. And while it is important to have our own revelation about things, it is critical to know that not every hard lesson needs to be learned from experience.

I understand that there is also that place in your inner person that will make you persist in going after what you want against every rational reason. There is something greater driving you, pushing you forward relentlessly until you reach your next, where every setback deepens your resolve to reach your goal. The question becomes, "Is it you, or is it God?" Are you in season or out of season in your pursuit?

There is a real tension between knowing when to dig in your heels and hold on or let go and free-fall into what God has waiting for you. The season you are in will tell you. When God gives you manna, stay on course. When He dries up everything around you, it is time to let go of your insistence and move on. In all things, walk with open hands. If you never make your dream or the things you desire an idol, you will always be in a position for things to work out for the good. But this is an aside.

Let's get back to all of the areas we experience with seasons that may surprise us based on lack of knowledge. The Bible tells us to pursue knowledge and *"love wisdom like a sister"* (Proverbs 7:4). I think I know why. It is only knowledge, wisdom, and understanding that will keep you centered as life unfolds. All these things come from God. There is a difference between worldly wisdom and divine impartation. Worldly wisdom draws from its own strength and rationale. It is its own source and can shift at any moment. Divine wisdom comes from above and is relevant in every season because it has a bird's-eye view of life. It sees the beginning from the end and provides answers for every twist and turn in life.

While visiting my ophthalmologist, I told him I had started using reading glasses to see fine print. He calmly told me, "Um hmm that's what happens after forty." I asked, "Who told you I was forty!?" He answered, "Well, your face didn't tell me, but your eyes did. It's rather common as we age." The words "as we age" rang in my ears long after my appointment. I hadn't thought about aging up to that point. I felt the same. I looked the same. My brain felt like twenty even though I was forty. But the season was upon me for things to be altered internally. My outlook on life was different. What used to matter didn't matter anymore. Even my taste in men had changed! I was in a different season of life without realizing it. Things were silently shifting within me and outside of me.

CHANGES WE GO THROUGH

I wish my mother had told me about aging. Perhaps she didn't because she appeared ageless for so very long. When I asked her why she hadn't told me about certain things, she said she hadn't thought about it. Now that she is in her late eighties with several different ailments she never thought she would experience, every now and then, she will bemoan the process of aging. But there are little things, like what happens to your neck and under your eyes. Little secrets on how to keep the wrinkles away. Menopause, or as I call it, "Man on pause." All these things were thrust upon me without my awareness! As we age, shifts take place in our bodies, whether we are male or female. Some develop stiffness. We get up and move a little slower, depending on our level of physical activity. Our bodies pay the price if we have rarely exercised.

Different health issues come into play. Doctors recommend specific tests for specific ages to make sure you keep a clean bill of health. Diet becomes more important because your body is no longer producing everything it used to in your younger years. Some people develop allergies or arthritis. The list of physical shifts and experiences goes on. It is a season of next that many fight against or try to deny is happening, which doesn't help.

Fact: For all nexts, adjustments need to be made to maintain a good quality of life.

In the season of aging physically, it's not enough to say, "If I knew then what I know now, I would have done things differently." Part of the art of mastering the shift is knowing how to adjust and follow through. Some determine they are on their way out, so they continue doing and eating what they always have with the rationale that they may as well enjoy themselves even though those habits are detrimental to them.

Don't run away from aging. Embrace it. Decide to gracefully accept and adjust your next. Find the excitement in the process of shifting your lifestyle to one that is conducive to the season you are in. Know you've earned the right to be where you are!

Although aging may come with challenges, it also comes with a plethora of blessings. There is a greater sense of self that we possess when we've experienced various intervals of life and found ourselves still standing. Hopefully, we've gained enough knowledge to make sounder decisions because of past experiences. We are no longer starting from scratch when we experience a setback. We possess greater peace because we've owned who we are and the season we are in while also settling unresolved issues.

There is nothing more unfortunate than watching someone fighting the season they are in by refusing to be realistic and or make the necessary adjustments. For some, aging is a strike against what they determine to be their identity. Athletes and actors in particular can really struggle with this. For many of them, their career depends on being youthful. When they see their season changing, they see it as a dead-end, while it could be just a transition that allows another facet of their talents and abilities to come to the forefront. Those who understand that it is never over find their next with grace. In some instances, their career flourishes even more because they choose to embrace where they are in the present and make it work for them.

The same can hold true for you. Embrace the reality that, in this season, you can't do what you did in the last season. See the end of the former season as the beginning of a new one with endless possibilities.

Many are experiencing aging on two levels—their own personal experience and that of aging parents who require extra care. Making the right choices for their care can be overwhelming and time-consuming. It is also traumatic to come to the realization that they are getting closer and closer to transitioning from this life to the next. Dementia and Alzheimer's disease are on the rise, and many see their parents slipping away from them before their very eyes as they turn inward to a place that can't be reached by those watching. Nothing can prepare you for a time when you become a stranger to the ones who nurtured you. And then one day, they are gone. You knew that death was a reality until it visited you, tearing your heart as you grasp the finality of their departure, and you have to accept that it's finally goodbye. Some never do, yet it is necessary. Again another season has come to a close.

Aging represents progression in our seasons. We move from infancy and innocence to childhood, curiosity, and learning to teenage years of experimentation and training to adulthood. The latter season includes entering the workforce, getting married for some, having a family, building a home, entering a profession, and creating a lasting legacy. Each season matures us into who we are and shapes how we live and leave our mark on the world. There is a season to give birth to ideas and dreams. There is a season to grow physically, spiritually, and mentally. There is a season to practice all that you have learned, to be productive and fruitful.

There is a season of rest. Even God rested—not out of exhaustion but out of appreciation for His creation. He took the time to survey and celebrate all that He had done. He didn't retire. The word *retirement* makes me think of getting tired all over again. Re-tire. I am not condemning retirement. However, I believe our latter season is about creating a legacy. After

God finished creating, He moved on to transforming mankind into a lasting image of Himself through the work of redemption and regeneration by His Spirit. To leave a legacy, the old need to teach the young and hand down their wisdom to the next generation. It's called leaving your fingerprints behind. Because ultimately, the next season will be your departure from earth to move on to your next.

SHIFTING TIMES

Our lives are like sand on the beach, always shifting beneath the tide. The sea washes away the last impressions, leaving a clean palate to create new ones. As we age, we have various relationships, which also have their seasons—spring, winter, summer, and fall. The first flush of romance feels like spring, new, beautiful, and hopeful. Summer is the building passion that burns in our hearts and makes us say, "Yes, I want to spend the rest of my life with this person." Fall is a time for building and planting a future together. Winter may be a myriad of different occurrences—deep disappointments, tragedy striking in some way, devastating losses... Some make it through winter. Some do not.

The reality is that in every season, the weather is not always perfect. Rain doesn't make us hate spring; it simply makes us wait for the sunny day we believe is coming. As in the natural seasons, those who stay firm, making the necessary adjustments, make it through to better weather. I find it interesting that most happily married couples will say, "It wasn't always this way! We went through some stuff!" There is no such thing as a perfect, uneventful marriage. They are all tested at some point. The couples who lasted decided that even through setbacks, disappointments, and sometimes even infidelity, it was not the end, but just a detour to their next should they decide to continue the journey together.

Relationships can be seasonal or lifelong, but within each one, there will be shifts and changes, seasons of the heart. Every day will be different. Some days, you will like the person in your life and some days you won't. There will be seasons of disappointment, needs not being met, misunderstanding, offense, forgiveness, growth, and discovery, and seasons of romance, marriage, divorce, and widowhood. It all happens. Yet love and hope spring eternal. Shifting and changing. Never looking the same. None can be predicted. And whether it is anticipated or not, we must face the reality of each season and lean into it. Dress for it. And continue forward.

Every successful businessperson will tell you there are seasons you must endure in order to achieve your goals. Even the stock exchange has its seasons, a bear market in which stock prices are down and a bull market in which they are up. Some sell when prices drop; afraid to ride out the season, they may lose great dividends. Those who wait it out cash in on those same abandoned stocks when the market rises again. We've been taught to buy low and sell high, but some don't have the courage to wait out the fluctuations.

Even the world's wealthiest people have suffered great seasons of loss, yet they bounced back to sit on top of the world. They will tell you that the willingness to take risks and lean into adversity was key to shifting their season and making the losses work for them.

There are seasons for planting by investing in a business or dream, fertilizing when one has nurtured the right relationships, employees, or habits, seasons of maintaining new growth, and then seasons of pruning. Pruning is necessary to cut back the things that will hinder future growth.

BACK TO THE GARDEN

Corporations may go through change management to look at the business overall, determine what it is producing and what it is not, and figure out why. They may discover they need to let some employees go, hire new ones, or cut back some departments that aren't producing. They call it *trimming the fat* in order to become more streamlined, productive, and profitable. Some procedures may have to be redefined and shifted. Changes need to be made to increase efficiency and revenue. Yeah, sounds like life to me—professionally, personally, and yes, even spiritually.

It may be necessary to repot and trim a houseplant for it to grow taller, stronger, and more fruitful. Perhaps it doesn't look attractive at first, but the end result is beautiful. I remember passing a vineyard when the vines had been pruned. It looked pretty barren and pitiful, but by the end of the season, the vines were loaded with lush, beautiful grapes, a wonderful illustration of the benefits of pruning. Instead of fearing the process, we should joyfully anticipate the end result. Be willing to lose it all to gain it all. Loss is never permanent; it is the gateway to your next.

We all need a season of reinvention. Nothing stays the same. It can't. That is called stagnation, which leads to death. Those who are most successful are those who can morph and reinvent themselves in the face of changing times. When the COVID-19 pandemic hit, many had to change the way they did business, church, and their personal lives in order to stay afloat under the flood of uncertainty. Businesses discovered that workers were actually more productive when they worked from home. This has shifted the commerce and occupational landscape. New parameters have been set. The work week now looks drastically different for many. How we do business has been revolutionized and forever changed.

A NEW APPROACH

As I noted previously, churches discovered that attendance went up online. For many, so did giving, as their audience increased beyond their regular church attendees to reach the world. With nowhere to go and endless numbers seeking answers and hope, the church had a captive audience and became a production as it devised ways to make its online presence look appealing to the masses. Those who never attended church previously now did so from the comfort of their homes. Some watched more than one service. Viewers now had the freedom to scroll and discover new teachers. For me, this meant devising an online MMH Hangout space where men and women from all over the world came online every week to network and hear great speakers, thanks to the amazing invention of Zoom. The hindrance of not being able to be physically present with people did not deter me from reaching out to them on the airwaves at a time when the need for encouragement was at an all-time high. People found new ways to connect. Life will never be the same again in any sector because of the innovations that were created at a time when the world was seemingly locked down.

Fact: We are a resilient people. Necessity is definitely the mother of invention. The various seasons we encounter demand that we find new ways of functioning and expressing ourselves. Seasons accelerate our capacity to live life to the fullest, forcing us to discover new pathways and the means to continue our journey.

In the face of gasoline crises, the electric car has been invented. This did not come about earlier because there was no urgency, but now, it's a different season. Various expressions of solar power are now used to help those facing energy shortages. The determination to survive will place a demand on our creativity that will birth amazing solutions if we persist in the exercise of life.

SEASONAL SENSITIVITY

Being wise can help us navigate through economic seasons in the world. Though they are universal, they impact us personally. Many live paycheck to paycheck with no foresight toward the future. Many have found themselves in their later years with no retirement nest egg because they didn't plan well. No one told them to invest in their future while they were enjoying their present. Historically, there have been seasons of great affluence and then economic depressions. One cannot always foresee them, but they are inevitable. It is a part of the cycle of life. There are fluctuations in every area. Although God has promised that we will flourish in the midst of famine, we need to operate in His wisdom in order for this to occur.

Even nature is aware of the seasons. It anticipates and prepares for them by saving provisions for the season of scarcity. How much more should we be aware of the seasons and prepare for them? Summer for ants, squirrels, beavers, mice, and some species of birds is not just a time of enjoyment; they are also diligently storing up what will not be available in winter.

When you are young, there is a tendency to think that things will continue as they are forever. As you mature, you realize that is not an accurate assessment. Things change. Life happens. Shift happens. Can you pivot? Can you handle change? And are you prepared for it?

Finally, let us not ignore the seasons of the soul—the joyful times, when faith is high and everything seems to be going your way, and the dark times of feeling forsaken and alone, wondering if God hears you. As you mature in your faith, you find a balance between faith and fear, joy and despair, peace and chaos, confidence and doubt. However, depending on the trial that you face, you can revisit a season that you thought you had gotten past.

The fact that someone as powerful as Elijah the prophet could suffer a bout of anxiety, depression, and even have suicidal thoughts is mind-blowing. He was having a real bleak season of the soul after Jezebel threatened to kill him. Fleeing in fear, Elijah *"prayed that he might die. 'I have had enough,* Lord,*' he said. 'Take my life, for I am no better than my ancestors who have already died'"* (1 Kings 19:4).

Job, another famous biblical person who lost everything, rued the day he was born, saying, *"Why wasn't I born dead? Why didn't I die as I came from the womb?"* (Job 3:11). Yet he was full of knowledge on the ways of God, and people sought his counsel.

Jesus had a dark season in the garden of Gethsemane as He faced the awful task of becoming sin for us. (See 2 Corinthians 5:21.) Dreading the impending separation from His Father, which had never happened before, He told His disciples, *"My soul is crushed with grief to the point of death"* (Matthew 26:38).

LET TIME HAVE ITS WAY

We all experience these dark seasons.

Don't beat yourself up; just talk to yourself, discipline yourself to stop, and do the heart work to discover why you are there. Keep in mind that this too shall pass, but what you do in this season is critically important. Whatever you do, don't make important decisions now. Emotions can deceive you and cause you to write checks that bounce or make commitments that you will regret. How do you navigate during these times, which can push all your buttons and hit so close to home that you lack clarity? Stop. Never be in a hurry to resolve an issue. Sometimes, time does its best work when you do nothing.

Cry out to God. Be still and know that He *is* God. He likes you. In fact, He loves you and has the best of intentions for you always. Seek counsel if you must. Don't be ashamed to say you need help. Don't try to do life alone.

We were made for community. We were not created for isolation. And yet pride creates a prison that lengthens the term of the dark places we visit. Light and truth are our sources of freedom and renewal. As we reach out to others and get the help and support we need, we are empowered to make it.

There are times when only God can do the work. When Elijah was depressed, he rested in the presence of God. Ravens and angels gave him food and water. (See 1 Kings 17:6; 19:6.) God strengthened him to continue his journey. No excuses were made or accepted. Time was given for Elijah's recovery—but not for him to wallow in pity, nurse his fears, and rehearse the events that made him feel the way he did. God reassured him that he was not alone or abandoned and sent help to assist him.

When we are absorbing a lot of blowback, negativity, or pressure, we need to take the time we need to mend, but also to accept aid.

The momentum of major accomplishments can lead to depletion if we are not careful to pace ourselves. Our bodies have an inner fuse box that can shut down when we are overloaded, leading to symptoms of depression, anxiety, and burnout. It makes us stop in our tracks. We don't feel like doing anything. Some people even lose their appetite! The body is screaming, "Time out!" as it seeks recovery and refueling. We can only avoid overheating and imploding by pacing ourselves in the heat of the season. Before Elijah contemplated suicide, he had just experienced summer! He had defeated a horde of prophets, outran a chariot, and basically operated at superhuman capacity. (See 1 Kings 18:40, 46.) I'm sure it was a heady experience at the time, yet he quickly found himself in winter because of what he had accomplished in summer. It brought a different threat to his life that caused him to run for cover and question God.

A famous actor who disgraced himself publicly on one of the greatest nights of his life said he had been counseled that attacks will come when we are at our highest moments. This was said after he failed the test miserably. Before or after our summer, we are sometimes blindsided by things that can get us caught in a tailspin. I will go further to say that this is the pattern, going and coming. If we consider the storms of spring leading into summer, we clearly see massive activity designed to make us abort our harvest and keep us from getting to our next season.

The transitional season is always tenuous and fragile. Anything can happen. As King Solomon noted, *"The love apples are in bloom"* (Song of

Songs 7:13 TPT), but *"our vines have tender grapes"* (Song of Songs 2:15 KJV), vulnerable to the elements internally and externally.

Your mind can do more damage than outward influences or voices. You must gain personal clarity and press through this. Once you get to summer, enjoy it but don't cast off discipline. It will be a requirement for sustaining and maintaining what you acquire and achieve.

IN THE SPIRIT

Our spiritual element is unseen by the natural eye but obvious to the discerning. In this life, there are two teams—one cheering us on toward our next, and the other working against it. Persistence, emotional intelligence, an understanding of the process, and a sense of purpose are the pillars that will keep us rooted until we flourish and bear fruit in our season.

It's important to listen to the right voice that speaks clearer than your circumstances to keep you in a state of peace regardless of your season. This voice will give you a vision beyond where you are standing and what you are up against. The voice of God will give you direction and shed light in the darkness of uncertainty during shifting and trying times. This intimate connection will keep you and give you the strength to pivot, turn, change direction, and if need be, get from where you presently are to your next.

Oh yes, there will be many voices, many opinions. My mother used to say, "Opinions are like people's behinds; everyone has one. Some are more attractive than others." Voices can be sources of illusion and confusion. Still your soul. Seek a quiet place. Listen to the *"still small voice"* (1 Kings 19:12 KJV) that will counsel you on the way forward. Lean into the arms and voice of God, which will never steer you wrong. Sometimes His direction will not make sense but it will always bear fruit if you obey.

Some things don't reveal themselves immediately. Like Noah building the ark before the flood. The next was coming, and he was ready, while others scoffed at what he was doing. Abraham didn't know where he was going, but he determined he would know it when he got there.

The bottom line for all of the seasons is that each one will never be the same and will require a different kind of faith, different responses, and different things to happen. Staying open and flexible to change is required.

Your insistence that things stay the same will hamper your progress and your ability to get your desired results. The Lord of the seasons is the one who can best tell you how to navigate every twist and turn in life and ultimately help you to reap and enjoy your harvest with the anticipation of yet another wonderful next!

WHEN SHIFT HAPPENS

It is inevitable that changes and shifts will occur, but we have options in how we respond. Let us always keep our desired outcome in mind when we are hit with the birthing pangs of change. There is a time for clinging to what once fed us and knowing when to release it. For the Israelites in Egypt, what once was the land of refuge turned into a place of bondage. Knowing when to leave is as critical as perceiving when to enter and how long to remain. Seeing every season as an opportunity rather than an inconvenience will empower us to live our best life in every season.

MINDSHIFT

+ Out of all the seasons mentioned, which one are you experiencing now?

+ What are you most concerned about?

+ What are your options for moving forward?

+ What do you need to do to make the best of this season?

+ What new mindset do you need to embrace to avoid repeating former mistakes?

HINDSIGHT

In retrospect, you should examine past behavior patterns in former seasons that are similar to the one you are presently in. This becomes a time to examine if former responses served you and what needs to be changed now. Also, based on what you have learned, decide how you will pace yourself moving forward.

Ask yourself this question: What is my ultimate desired outcome and what do I need to do differently to make that happen?

THE NEXT PRAYER

But you must continue to believe this truth and stand firmly in it. Don't drift away from the **assurance** *you received when you heard the Good News.* (Colossians 1:23)

Dear heavenly Father, I praise You because You know the beginning from the end. You see all. You know all. You know the way that I take. You have written all my days in Your book, and You are not surprised by any of the events that have taken place. When I come to the end of myself, help me find the beginning of You. It is in You that I will find my next. Help me to remember that. When I am tempted to give up hope and think that it is over and that my best is behind me, remind me of Your promises. Clarify my vision to see there is always something beyond where I live. Remind me of the assurance You have given me for life. Help me to stand firmly in what I know but forget from time to time. Bring me back to myself and renew my expectation of the things to come. I am believing You for my next, in the name of Christ Jesus. Amen.

If money and time were no object, what would you be doing with your life?

_____

_____

_____

_____

What would you like your next to look like?

_____

_____

_____

_____

Write your faith confession here:

_____

_____

_____

_____

THIRTEEN

ALL SHIFTS MATTER

Take a look around you. There has been a shift in the world that has us set on an accelerated course of major changes. The world went from a year of lockdown to an intermediate return to somewhat full activity, but it has never fully regained its previous momentum. However, on the other hand, things have revved up to a fever pitch as the entire world wrestles with its economy, political leadership, supply shortages, the deaths of major influencers in our world—you name it! Several political leaders have been forced to resign, and people have taken to the streets to lift their voices in protest over numerous issues. There is tension in the air. People are angry, disgruntled, and downright fed up. The old grace seems to have disappeared as a more vocal generation refuses to take things lying down. Whether you see this as good or bad, it is an indication of shifting times.

Plagues and pestilence, severe weather conditions, political unrest, economic uncertainty, people casting off restraint, racism, hatred and bloodshed, religious animosity and persecution, wars and rumors of wars... sounds familiar, right? The birth pangs are beginning signs of the times;

the final season is closer than ever, where we will all move on to a greater next.

Eternity is not a reality to many, so they live shortsighted lives engorged with urgency to get everything *now*—when this is all that there is becomes the prevailing mindset. However, to find a utopia on earth is the height of unrealistic thinking. That is what awaits in the eternal next.

Here is where we must be sensitive and aware of the shifting culture around us. When we walk in awareness, we know where to step, what to do or not do, and what to say or not say. We recognize critical moments for when we should show up. We are able to focus on what really matters and keep a clear vision of our end goal. The things shifting about us should not influence our purpose or stop us from fulfilling the assignment we were created for. The mission doesn't change but how we accomplish it may. Refusing to adjust our methods to be relevant to the place we are in and the people we are called to affect is like insisting on speaking English in a foreign country that speaks another language.

What you are saying may be great, but if no one understands you, what is the point? How do you make an impact? This may cause discomfort for many. People want change but don't necessarily want to change. Sounds crazy, doesn't it? But the way to tap into your next is to remain relevant in every shift and season.

STAYING RELEVANT

So how do we become purposefully relevant without compromising? In a world where people are now penalized for being politically incorrect, making a slip of the tongue, or not getting the letters and pronouns right, how do we navigate with grace and love to make a positive difference? Free speech no longer means free opinions to some. We must be sensitive, read the room, measure our words and responses, and be discerning of timing so that what we say is well-placed and received in the spirit in which it was given. We need to recognize that not everything requires an answer. There is a time to speak and a time to be silent.

More than ever, one has to be conscious of the season. Revisit where you were for priceless lessons learned, reposition yourself to master the new terrain before you, and rebrand to appeal to a broader audience at work, at home, in your community, and in your interpersonal relationships. Your territory, which you can influence in ways you do not yet know, is being expanded. Life is not about fame; it is about enhancing the quality of the lives you've been given access to. Social media is doing a number on youth and even adults. The pressure to live unrealistic lives is real due to false imagery. Here is your opportunity to reflect the power of being real and the value of authenticity. It means you will be going against the grain of the world system. It takes courage to stand firm in the face of opposing voices, but it is the pathway to your next.

Know what to take to heart and what things are mere distractions from what matters. Let me say that again. Some things are mere distractions—smoke and mirrors designed to take you off point and out of your season. One wrong reaction can set you back and rob you of the future you saw, all because you didn't read the room, didn't sense the atmosphere, or missed reading between the lines.

Know the culture you are addressing, since it can shift from country to country, state to state, city to city, business to business, church to church, room to room, and even person to person. Jesus had a knack for knowing His audience. He understood the season and what mindset prevailed because of it. This was how He was able to be relevant no matter who He was talking to. He spoke to fishermen in fishing terms, which mattered to them. He was able to connect to the masses without offending anyone… except for religious people. Ah, those wonderful religious people. He didn't really care about shaking them up. They were not His audience.

Know your audience. Trying to please the wrong audience can keep you from reaching your next. This applies to every area of life. If you are considering marriage, you need to know your fiancé's family culture. It may be different from yours. You may need to make some adjustments. At the very least, you should have an awareness of what awaits you. When you get a new job, you need to know the company's culture. What are their values? Those things will impact your ability to be successful in work. Across the board, be aware.

Things are changing quickly. In order to remain relevant and impactful, you must be aware of the dynamics at play around you, whether you like them or not, whether you feel they are right or not. It is the present reality. It may not matter to you, but it matters to someone. Eventually, everything everywhere affects everyone at some time. Chickens do come home to roost, and it never seems to be a convenient time when it happens. Be in the know so that you can navigate well.

LOCATE YOURSELF

Our spirits need to operate like a GPS, able to chart out where the traffic jams are so we can avoid getting stuck. We need that internal ability at this time. God is all-knowing, therefore because of the connection Jesus had with His Father, He was always well-informed about who and what He was dealing with. Because of this, He was successful in His mission of adding to the kingdom of God. He had a great following because of His ability to connect with men and women from all walks of life. He was the king of reinvention and has remained relevant to the present day because He became the solution for what was needed at the time—and for all time. He went from being King of Glory in the creation to mortal Man and teacher, then became our Savior, Redeemer, and Intercessor. He will return as the reigning King. In the meantime, His Spirit is with us to help us navigate on a daily basis as a Counselor, Comforter, and the One who empowers us for whatever we need. He anticipates our next and equips us to handle it.

Joseph was sold into slavery by his brothers, but he was able to rise above the bonds of slavery and master his next in a beautiful story that doesn't tell us about all of the pain or trauma he suffered. (See Genesis 37:28; 39:20.) After being betrayed by his brothers, falsely accused, and imprisoned in a culture that didn't even speak his language, Joseph kept going and made the best of his situation until he reached his next. How? By being the solution to the needs of the people he served. From Potiphar to the prison warden to finally Pharaoh, he kept rising to the top in every circumstance. (See Genesis 39:2–6; 39:21–23; 40:37–44.) Finally, he became the right-hand man of Pharaoh, all because he looked beyond his personal pain and setback to be the answer to someone else's need.

Your next depends on your ability to meet present needs. In your place of business, your interpersonal relationships, family, and social gatherings, take the time to see people where they are. Get a feel for the season they are in, their culture, and their needs.

What do they need? More than ever, people need truth laced with love and authenticity. They just want something that is real. When we fail to be authentic in our encounters with others, the connection is lost. They may not even know why they couldn't receive from us because it's spiritual.

All shifts matter because, hopefully, they are shaping you into the person you were created to be, a person who will bring a positive and lasting impact to those divinely assigned to your circle. Your next has everything to do with the lives of others besides yourself. Your life is bigger than you. While you are anticipating your next, someone needs you to show them the way to their next.

We are all in this race called life together. We must be able to pass the baton off to the next person and keep it moving! The seeds you plant now will bear harvest not just in your own next but in someone else's. For this core reason, you should never give up or give in. Everything in life leads to a next. You got fired? Next! Your partner left you? Next! You just lost that deal? Missed out on lots of money? Didn't get that opportunity you thought was yours? Next! You just missed that exit? Next! Even God had a next. When He lost man to sin, He shifted into His plan to redeem the world.

A friend of mine who's a journalist came to visit me in Ghana. He arrived with trunks of equipment to cover his journey. Four iPhones, four drones, and five cameras. He had to have at least a hundred batteries. When I commented on all of his stuff, he replied, "I have learned to always be prepared for anything! You never know what will happen." Sure enough, during one of his adventures, the canoe he was in overturned, and he lost a drone, a phone, and a camera. The ocean took them away. It didn't stop him. He just said, "Next!" and whipped out his backup camera, drone, and phone.

I hope you get what I'm saying. Your next depends on you—on your mindset, outlook, state of readiness, and ability to think and move quickly on your feet. Don't get stuck where you are! Don't let what happened paralyze you. More awaits. It's called your next!

There is always a next! And as the queen of Sheba said after visiting King Solomon, "The half of it has not been told!" (See 1 Kings 10:7.) So take your eyes off the immediate. Develop long-term vision to see beyond where you are. Visualize your next and have a succession plan for every area of your life. No matter what, remember that everything in life has an expiration date.

As I've shared, I had to adjust to leaving the familiar and moving to three continents, an island, and two major cities. I've lost jobs, the love of my life to death, and a parent. Lost money. Lost my home. Three of my dogs have died. I've lost great opportunities. Lost the ability to function on my own for a period of time. These are just a few things that have devastated me. The pain seemed as if it would never subside. I've been sidelined time and time again by the unthinkable, but through it all, I have learned that nothing lasts forever—with the exception of eternity. Everything else comes to pass.

You have endless options, but you will only see them if you believe in one small and powerful word: Next!

WHEN SHIFT HAPPENS

When shift happens in your life, it is not an indication of failure or a judgment of how you've lived thus far. It is merely the push you need to move forward, to cast off old thoughts and habits to help you turn the corner of life, step up, and embrace a whole new season. Yet in order for that to happen, you need to make informed choices in a way that will be relevant to your current environment. Remember, you get to master how impactful you will be based on your ability to connect with others and the legacy you create. You will never reach your next alone.

MINDSHIFT

+ Who are you assigned to? For what purpose?
+ What culture are you dealing with?
+ Where do you find resistance?
+ What shift do you need to make to be relevant?
+ What is your succession plan?

HINDSIGHT

Life is a series of nexts. When we embrace this reality, we can shift easily and roll with the punches that may assault us. There is no specified number of changes ahead. Life is an education in which we move on to the next grade when we've learned the lesson and passed the test. Unlike the world's educational system, in life, we get as many chances as we need to live, learn, and move forward when we've acquired knowledge. Everyone's journey is personal yet progressive. There is no rush. The ultimate goal is not to run headlong through a series of nexts for the sake of racing through experiences and avoiding teachable moments, but to arrive at the ultimate next, which is more meaningful and lasting—completing the race and finishing well. Then we will hear God tell us, "*Well done, my good and faithful servant*" (Matthew 25:21) as we enter into the final next, that continuum of eternal joy and pleasures evermore.

Ask yourself this question: What do you want people to say about you when you've moved on to your next?

THE NEXT PRAYER

"For I know the plans I have for you," says the Lord. *"They are plans for good and not for disaster, to give you a future and a hope."*
(Jeremiah 29:11)

Dear heavenly Father, sometimes it's hard to believe that You care about what I care about. I know You collect my tears in a bottle and You love me with an everlasting love, but sometimes life tells me otherwise. And yet I cling desperately to Your promise, waiting for You to show Your hand. I know my timing is not Yours, which is the thing that really stretches my faith. I am like a child on a very long car trip who asks repeatedly, "Are we there yet?" Thank You for Your patience and Your reassurances when I am scratching the bottom of my faith. I will choose to trust You. I will choose to wait on You. I will choose to let go of taking my life into my hands. I will run into Your arms and stay there until You complete what You have begun in me and for me. Help me to wait in joyful expectation in the name of Christ Jesus. Amen.

What makes you struggle with waiting?

_____

_____

_____

_____

What do you want most?

_____

_____

_____

_____

Write your faith confession here:

_____

_____

_____

_____

Can you not discern this new day of destiny breaking forth around you? The early signs of my purposes and plans are bursting forth. The budding vines of new life are now blooming everywhere. The fragrance of their flowers whispers, "There is change in the air."

(Song of Songs 2:13 TPT)

ABOUT THE AUTHOR

Known as the "queen of reinvention and empowerment," Michelle McKinney Hammond has authored over forty books selling over two million copies worldwide, including *What to Do Until Love Finds You*; *The Diva Principle*; *Sassy, Single and Satisfied*; *101 Ways to Get and Keep His Attention*; and *Secrets of an Irresistible Woman*.

Born in London, England, Michelle spent her childhood in Barbados, West Indies, and Muskegon, Michigan. Although she says she was "an ugly duckling" and bullied as a child, by high school, she was acting and singing in lead roles in both community and school productions.

After high school, Michelle moved to Chicago and graduated from the Ray-Vogue College of Design, now the Illinois Institute of Art. During a trip to Ghana to meet her biological father's family for the first time, she was deeply influenced by her paternal grandmother, a devoutly religious woman who spent several hours a day in prayer. Later, after returning to the U.S., Michelle became a committed Christian.

She joined the Chicago-based Burrell Advertising, where she eventually became an associate creative director. Michelle had a successful career in advertising as an art director, writer, and producer, with clients such as Coca-Cola USA, McDonald's, Procter and Gamble, and General Motors Company. She received numerous awards for her work, including a U.S. Television Award, more than thirty Creative Excellence in Black Advertising awards, a Windy Award, and bronze and silver International Television Association Philo Awards.

In 1995, Michelle suffered a devastating leg injury after being hit by a car. She was bedridden for a year and a half, but the accident marked a spiritual turning point for her. She decided to pursue a new career helping single Christian women find a healthy, fulfilling life, with or without a husband. Her first bestseller, *What to Do Until Love Finds You*, was published in 1997.

Since then, Michelle has launched a multifaceted career as speaker, singer, producer, actress, relationship expert, and life coach, reaching men and women from all walks of life.

Michelle is the president of U.S.-based Michelle McKinney Hammond (MMH) Ministries and DivaCor LLC, and the chairman of Ghana-based Belmont Resources, Meridien Securities, and Akwaaba Leisure Ltd. She was awarded an honorary doctorate of ministry from American Bible University.

She has recorded four solo CDs—*It's Amazing, Let's Go In, Come Let Us Worship*, and *With Love*. She is also the visionary, pastor, and lead singer of Relevance, a unique music ministry based in Ghana, West Africa, where she makes her home. Relevance focuses on moving the church beyond walls and taking worship to the streets with *rockspiration*, a fusion of rock, reggae, jazz, and African percussion. They have released three CDs, entitled *Forever, The Greatest Gift*, and *For Love's Sake*, with a fourth CD set for release in 2023.

She cohosted and won an Emmy for her work on the Total Living Network's Emmy Award-winning television talk show *Aspiring Women* for ten years and Tri-State Christian Television's *3D Woman* for eight seasons.

Michelle most recently appeared in Roma Downey and Mark Burnett's productions of *Women of the Bible* on Lifetime and *A.D., The Bible Continues*. She presently does inspirational "Truth But Fair" segments on their new network lightworkers.com and Light TV. Michelle has also acted in several African soap operas and movies.

She has appeared on countless other radio and television shows, including Bill Maher's *Politically Incorrect*, NBC's *The Other Half*, *The 700 Club*, Daystar, Huntley Street, TBN, BET's *Oh Drama*, and *The Michael Baisden Show*. She has also been featured as a regular relationship segment host on Chicago's *WGN Morning News* and Fox's *Fox and Friends*.

Michelle has been featured in *Today's Christian Woman*, *Precious Times*, *The Plain Truth*, *Gospel Today*, *Essence*, *Ebony*, *Jet*, *Black Enterprise Magazine*, *Chicago Tribune*, and *The New York Times*.

To connect with Michelle or find more resources, visit michellehammond.com.